The Value-Added Tax

Studies of Government Finance: Second Series

TITLES PUBLISHED

Who Pays the Property Tax? A New View, by Henry J. Aaron

Federal Tax Reform: The Impossible Dream? by George F. Break and Joseph A. Pechman

The Individual Income Tax (rev. ed.), by Richard Goode

Inflation and the Income Tax, Henry J. Aaron, Editor

Federal Tax Policy (3d ed.), by Joseph A. Pechman

Financing State and Local Governments (3d ed.), by James A. Maxwell and J. Richard Aronson

Federal Budget Policy (3d ed.), by David J. Ott and Attiat F. Ott

Comprehensive Income Taxation, Joseph A. Pechman, Editor

A Voluntary Tax? New Perspectives on Sophisticated Estate Tax Avoidance, by George Cooper

Must Corporate Income Be Taxed Twice? by Charles E. McLure, Jr.

What Should Be Taxed: Income or Expenditure? Joseph A. Pechman, Editor

Financing Government in a Federal System, by George F. Break

The Economics of Taxation, Henry J. Aaron and Michael J. Boskin, Editors

How Taxes Affect Economic Behavior, Henry J. Aaron and Joseph A. Pechman, Editors

The Value-Added Tax: Lessons from Europe, Henry J. Aaron, Editor

The Value-Added Tax: Lessons from Europe

HENRY J. AARON
Editor

Studies of Government Finance

THE BROOKINGS INSTITUTION

WASHINGTON, D.C.

Library of Congress Cataloging in Publication data:

Main entry under title:

The Value-added tax.

(Studies of government finance. Second series)

Includes index.

1. Value-added tax—Europe—Addresses, essays, lectures. 2. Value-added tax—United States—Addresses, essays, lectures. I. Aaron, Henry J. II. Brookings Institution. III. Series.

HJ5715.E9V29 336.2'714'094 81-38475

ISBN 0-8157-0028-8 AACR2

ISBN 0-8157-0027-X (pbk.)

9 8 7 6 5 4 3 2 1

THE BROOKINGS INSTITUTION is an independent organization devoted to nonpartisan research, education, and publication in economics, government, foreign policy, and the social sciences generally. Its principal purposes are to aid in the development of sound public policies and to promote public understanding of issues of national importance.

The Institution was founded on December 8, 1927, to merge the activities of the Institute for Government Research, founded in 1916, the Institute of Economics, founded in 1922, and the Robert Brookings Graduate School of Economics and Government, founded in 1924.

The Board of Trustees is responsible for the general administration of the Institution, while the immediate direction of the policies, program, and staff is vested in the President, assisted by an advisory committee of the officers and staff. The by-laws of the Institution state: "It is the function of the Trustees to make possible the conduct of scientific research, and publication, under the most favorable conditions, and to safeguard the independence of the research staff in the pursuit of their studies and in the publication of the results of such studies. It is not a part of their function to determine, control, or influence the conduct of particular investigations or the conclusions reached."

The President bears final responsibility for the decision to publish a manuscript as a Brookings book. In reaching his judgment on the competence, accuracy, and objectivity of each study, the President is advised by the director of the appropriate research program and weighs the views of a panel of expert outside readers who report to him in confidence on the quality of the work. Publication of a work signifies that it is deemed a competent treatment worthy of public consideration but does not imply endorsement of conclusions or recommendations.

The Institution maintains its position of neutrality on issues of public policy in order to safeguard the intellectual freedom of the staff. Hence interpretations or conclusions in Brookings publications should be understood to be solely those of the authors and should not be attributed to the Institution, to its trustees, officers, or other staff members, or to the organizations that support its research.

Foreword

AMONG the hardy perennials of American economics is the question of whether the United States should adopt a value-added tax. At least since the 1960s scattered organizations and elected officials have urged that the United States take the trail blazed by France and later followed by other countries in Europe and elsewhere and adopt this new form of taxation. In 1980 leaders of the two major tax-writing committees of Congress endorsed the value-added tax. Then, as previously, interest shifted; congressional attention now centers on how best to curtail taxation and government spending.

Faced in 1982 and later years with the prospect of large government deficits, public officials and private citizens are not only continuing to look at ways to cut spending, but some are also talking about how to collect more revenue, perhaps through the value-added tax. This book contributes to an understanding of the place of value-added taxation in public finance by reporting on European experience. To what extent have the claims of advocates and the fears of critics been validated? Is the value-added tax more neutral than alternative taxes? Does it promote saving? Is it simpler to administer than other taxes? Has it helped foreign countries with their balance of payments? Is it regressive? Does it promote inflation? While there is no guarantee that the United States would make all of the correct decisions—or all of the mistakes—that other countries have made, it is nevertheless prudent and desirable for Americans to learn from others.

For that reason the Brookings Institution organized a conference of tax experts in October 1980 to review papers on the experience of six European countries with the value-added tax. The papers in this book are abridgments of the papers presented at that conference. The introductory chapter by editor Henry Aaron is based on the conference discussion of the papers.

Henry J. Aaron is a senior fellow in the Brookings Economic Studies program and professor of economics at the University of Maryland. The manuscript was edited by Elizabeth H. Cross. Its factual content was verified by Penelope Harpold, and the index was prepared by Diana Regenthal. Secretarial assistance was provided by Kathleen Elliott Yinug.

The project was supported with funds provided by the German Marshall Fund of the United States. This is the fifteenth volume in the second series of Brookings Studies of Government Finance. Both series are devoted to examining issues of taxation and public policy.

The views expressed in this book are those of the authors and should not be ascribed to the German Marshall Fund or to the trustees, officers, or other staff members of the Brookings Institution.

BRUCE K. MACLAURY
President

September 1981
Washington, D.C.

Contents

Tables

HENRY J. AARON

Introduction and Summary

FOR CLOSE TO twenty years interest in the value-added tax has waxed and waned in the United States but never quite disappeared. During 1979 and 1980 Senator Russell Long and Representative Al Ullman, chairmen of the two leading congressional tax-writing committees, indicated support for the tax, and one proposed sweeping legislation that would have created a value-added tax yielding $115 billion to be used for reducing the personal and corporation income taxes and the payroll tax.[1] Two major accounting firms have published guides to the value-added taxes of European, African, South American, and Asian nations.[2] Within the past year the U.S. Treasury Department and the General Accounting Office have issued reports reviewing European experience with the value-added tax.[3]

Why has interest in the value-added tax persisted and grown during the

I am grateful to Sijbren Cnossen for supplying data for table 1.

1. Al Ullman, chairman of the House Committee on Ways and Means, sponsored H.R. 5665, the Tax Restructuring Act of 1979, a bill that would have imposed a value-added tax with a basic rate of 10 percent, yielding $115 billion in 1981. Hearings were held on November 8, 14, and 15, 1979. After making certain changes in the proposed legislation, Mr. Ullman on April 2, 1980, introduced H.R. 7015, the Tax Restructuring Act of 1980. No hearings were held on this, and Ullman subsequently withdrew his value-added tax proposal. He was defeated for reelection in 1980.

2. *VAT in Other Countries: An Arthur Andersen and Co. Study* (Chicago: Arthur Andersen and Co., 1980); *Value Added Tax* (New York: Price Waterhouse, 1979).

3. George N. Carlson, *Value Added Tax: European Experience and Lessons for the United States,* Department of the Treasury, Office of Tax Analysis, October 1980; Comptroller General, *Report to the Congress of the United States: The Value Added Tax in the European Economic Community* (General Accounting Office, December 5, 1980).

past couple of years? How valid are the claims made for the superiority of this form of taxation? Are they supported by the experience of nations that have adopted it? What special circumstances in the United States would make the value-added tax more or less attractive than it is in other countries?

To help answer these questions the Brookings Institution convened an international conference of economists, lawyers, and accountants to examine the experience of six European countries with the value-added tax and to draw lessons from that experience for the United States. This book summarizes the papers presented at the conference and the issues raised during the conference discussion.

What Is the Value-Added Tax?

Value added is the difference between the value of a firm's sales and the value of the purchased material inputs used in producing goods sold. Value added is also equal to the sum of wages and salaries, interest payments, and profits before tax earned by a firm. The value-added tax in Europe is a proportional tax levied on a sum equal to value added less purchases of investment goods.

To illustrate, assume that Firm A buys no material inputs, but it hires labor and makes a profit on sales valued at 20; Firm B buys all of Firm A's output and produces output worth 50; Firm C buys all of Firm B's output and produces goods that it sells to consumers for 100. Then value added by Firms A, B, and C are, respectively, 20, 30, and 50, and total value added is 100. A value-added tax of, say, 10 percent would bring a total revenue of 10—2 from Firm A, 3 from Firm B, and 5 from Firm C. If value added were unchanged, the net effect of such a tax would be to boost the price paid by final purchasers by 10, the sum of the taxes collected from all firms in the cycle of production and distribution.[4] In fact, the same revenue could be collected by a retail sales tax of 10 percent imposed only on sales to consumers by Firm C.

Implementing the Value-Added Tax

A number of important decisions must be made in designing a value-added tax. First, how should investment goods be treated in computing

4. A more realistic and complete illustration of the operation of a value-added tax in which all firms buy from and sell to each other and to the public and trade internationally is contained in the paper by Jean-Pierre Balladur and Antoine Coutière in this volume.

the tax? The legislature may permit businesses to treat investments exactly as they treat purchases of current inputs and to immediately deduct from sales the full value of investments made during the taxable period. Alternatively, firms may be permitted to deduct currently only the value of depreciation in the current production period. If the former method is used, the value-added tax is of the "consumption" type, because the tax base is the value of production in the current period less investment; if the latter method is used, the value-added tax is of the net income type, because the tax base equals output less depreciation, or the sum of consumption plus net investment.[5] The consumption type of value-added tax is the variety in use throughout Europe and most commonly discussed in the United States. The net income type of value-added tax has been supported for some time by various groups in Sweden.[6]

Second, how should the value-added tax be collected? Throughout Europe the "invoice" method is used. Each firm must collect value-added tax on all of its sales (unless they are exempt, an issue addressed below) and is entitled to a credit against its liability for taxes invoiced by its suppliers. Credit is allowed only if it is supported by invoices provided by suppliers. This method of administration is alleged to facilitate audits because each firm is required to supply evidence regarding taxes that should have been paid by all of its suppliers.[7] However, participants in the Brookings conference agreed that this advantage is not fully realized in practice and is unlikely to be fully realized because of the practical impossibility of checking all invoices. Also, much evasion occurs through the complete failure of some parties to report any aspect of a transaction.[8] On the other hand, there is a measure of self-policing in that (except at the retail stage) evasion by suppliers through understating tax collected

5. A third type of value-added tax disallows deductions for investment and for depreciation. It is referred to as the gross income type of value-added tax. No industrial nation now uses it or is considering its adoption.

6. See the paper by Göran Normann for further details.

7. Other methods of collection include the addition and the subtraction methods. Under the addition method, each firm must add up all elements in its value added: wages and salaries, interest, and profits. The subtraction method closely resembles the invoice method, but no invoices are required. For details on these matters, see Clara K. Sullivan, *The Tax on Value Added* (Columbia University Press, 1965).

8. If the invoice method was applied to the three firms mentioned above, Firm A would pay a tax of 2; Firm B would pay a gross tax of 5 but receive a credit of 2 for the tax paid by its supplier, Firm A, making a net liability of 3; and Firm C would pay a gross tax of 10 less a credit of 5, the gross tax on Firm B. Altogether, the government would receive a revenue of 10, or 10 percent of value added.

is counteracted by the purchasers' interest in ensuring that all tax paid is recorded. Similarly, evasion by purchasers in overstating tax paid runs counter to the interests of suppliers. Many conference participants expressed the view that the multistage character of the value-added tax, combined with the invoice method, make enforceable higher tax rates than would be possible under a retail sales tax.

Third, should all commodities be taxed at the same rate? This issue arises in two contexts. First, all the countries covered in this volume provide a complete rebate of all value-added taxes on exports, and impose tax on the full value of imports, without any credits for taxes paid abroad. This procedure, in combination with the deduction of investment, has the effect of taxing the consumption of domestic residents but imposes no burden on residents of other countries. This "destination principle" of taxation leaves each government free to set the level at which domestic consumption will be taxed without affecting the tax choices other governments face. As a practical matter, exports are freed from tax by imposing a zero rate on them; exporting firms thus pay zero tax on exports and receive a refund of all prior-stage taxes imposed in the production cycle of the exported commodities, and imports are taxed, putting them on the same footing as domestically produced goods. Second, zero or low rates can be used to lower tax rates on certain goods. All the countries covered in this book impose lower than normal effective rates of tax on certain classes of commodities, frequently essential items, consumed disproportionately by lower income groups; and most impose higher than normal rates on other goods, usually luxuries, consumed disproportionately by upper income groups.[9] One purpose of this variation in rates is to reduce tax burdens on low-income taxpayers and to increase them on the well-to-do in order to inject an element of progressivity into a tax that would otherwise be proportional with respect to consumption and regressive with respect to current money income.[10] Most countries introduced differentiated tax rates so that value-added tax burdens would resemble those of taxes they replaced. In other cases, differentiated rates are used for other purposes.

9. Sweden's value-added tax has only one rate, but the effective rate on some goods is reduced by including only a portion of value added. Only Denmark, not treated in this book, has a genuinely uniform tax.

10. The ratio of consumption to income declines with income, in part because the fraction of after-tax income saved rises with income and in part because the fraction of income paid in income tax rises with income.

All nations also exempt certain commodities from the value-added tax. Exemptions are awarded to small firms to avoid administrative nuisance and costly record-keeping; to certain classes of commodities that would be hard to tax, such as banking and financial services and owner-occupied housing; and to certain commodities classified as "social" goods, such as health services and education. An exempt firm is spared taxation on its sales, but it is also denied credit for taxes imposed on its inputs. If the exempt firm sells to households and has positive value added, exemption reduces net liabilities. If the exempt firm sells to other firms, then exemption increases tax burdens, because businesses that purchase exempt inputs have no credits to apply against their own tax liability. For example, if Firm B in the example described above was exempt, the government would collect not 10, but 12, in revenue: 2 from Firm A, nothing from Firm B because it is exempt, and 10 from Firm C; Firm C would be denied any credit because no tax was paid by its supplier, Firm B.[11] Similar effects may occur when small firms and farmers are exempted from the tax. However, to mitigate increases in the tax burden, some countries allow purchasers of farm products an imputed tax credit approximately equal to the weight of the value-added tax incorporated in agricultural production. For example, if Firm B was a farmer, the loss of the tax credit theoretically due him on his purchases from Firm A would be compensated by giving Firm C a credit of 2. Firm C's liability would then be 8, and the total revenue paid to the government 10, as in the normal case. Furthermore, in most European countries, the sale of important agricultural inputs such as fertilizers, seeds, and implements is taxed at lower than average rates.

The Basic Choice in Value-Added Tax Structure

Any nation considering the adoption of the value-added tax is confronted with a three-way trade-off. First, if all consumption is taxed at a single, uniform rate, the value-added tax appears neutral among alternative goods and services and does not distort consumer choice among them. This neutrality applies to consumption choices at each stage and to decisions about whether to consume now or later—the saving decision. The value-added tax cannot directly reach goods and services that do not pass through the market, the most important of which is leisure. However, economic theory shows that under certain conditions the taxation of

11. For a more detailed discussion of the complexities of exemption, see Balladur and Coutière, pp. 21–22 and table 1, below.

goods other than leisure at a uniform rate minimizes the inevitable distortions that any practical tax imposes.[12] These conditions are quite unlikely to be met, however.[13] Even in theory, therefore, a case can be made for the differentiation of tax rates on various commodities. In practice, the required differentiation would be hard to carry out, and the view persists that the potential neutrality (in other words, uniformity) of the value-added tax is one of its chief advantages.

If the value-added tax applied to all consumption goods at a uniform rate, the tax, by definition, would be proportional with respect to consumption, but it would be regressive with respect to annual income. The desire to reduce such regressivity or even to make the value-added tax progressive with respect to income leads to the taxation at lower than average rates of goods consumed disproportionately by low-income groups, or to ridding such goods of tax altogether by applying a zero rate to them, and to the taxation at higher than average rates of goods consumed disproportionately by high-income groups. The result, of course, would be the loss of neutrality as well as a reduction in regressivity.

Some nonneutrality is inevitable as a practical matter because not all consumption goods can be reached effectively by a value-added tax. The problem of taxing the services to households provided by banks and other financial institutions is intractable, because many of these services are not valued in money terms. Taxing the services of owner-occupied housing would be just as difficult politically under the value-added tax as it is under the personal income tax, but some tax would fall on residential construction, as deducting taxes on material inputs is not allowed. Exemption of such activities greatly simplifies administration.

The use of differentiated rates to lessen regressivity and the exemption of other commodities, on the other hand, complicate administration considerably. Firms selling both exempt and taxable goods must claim only the proportion of credits that is equal to the ratio of taxable to total sales. Defining classes of goods that will be subject to different tax rates and determining into which class a particular commodity should be placed

12. Lump-sum taxes always impose fewer distortions than any tax based on controllable economic behavior, but they are almost always regarded as unfair. The conditions necessary for a proportional or progressive tax on consumption to be optimal are stated in A. B. Atkinson and J. E. Stiglitz, "The Design of Tax Structure: Direct Versus Indirect Taxation," *Journal of Public Economics,* vol. 6 (July–August 1976), pp. 55–75.

13. A condition is that no change in the available quantity of any consumer good must affect the value of leisure time.

bedevils taxpayer and administrator alike with exercises in hairsplitting.[14] Moreover, rates must be differentiated only at the retail stage if the effects are to be clearly related to their cause. In short, efforts to improve the distribution of value-added tax burdens by taxing commodities at different rates inevitably complicate administration and compliance and destroy both neutrality and the advantages that uniformity may bring. A similar objective could be achieved by refundable credits calibrated on personal characteristics and measures of ability to pay.

European Experience

The experience with the value-added tax of each of the six countries described in the papers in this book is unique in many ways. In other respects, however, they share a common experience relevant to the choices that the United States would have to make if it chose to put a value-added tax into effect.

The most striking common element in the experience of all six countries is that each country used the value-added tax to replace an inferior sales tax that fell on most businesses. France, Italy, Germany, and the Netherlands had all collected substantial amounts of revenue for many years from taxes on gross turnover, an inferior form of taxation that falls with capricious unevenness on different commodities and that in some degree promotes vertical integration not justified on other grounds.[15] The United Kingdom had a kind of wholesale sales tax and an employment tax on services that in combination imposed burdens not very differently distributed from those of the value-added tax that succeeded them.[16] Sweden had a retail sales tax. As noted above, retail sales taxes and value-added taxes place similar patterns of burden on households, although they differ in the method and timing by which revenues are collected. The four nations with turnover taxes already had administrative procedures for dealing with most of the firms that became subject to the value-added tax, and a majority of the six designed the value-added tax to distribute tax burdens in roughly the same way as taxes that already existed did.

14. For illustrations of these problems, see Sijbren Cnossen, footnotes 5, 6, and 7; and Balladur and Coutière, footnote 4.

15. In the numerical example presented earlier, a 10 percent turnover tax would impose a liability of 2 on Firm A, 5 on Firm B, and 10 on Firm C, the same as the gross value-added tax liability. But no credits would be allowed, so that revenue would be 17. If the three firms merged, they could reduce the liability to 10.

16. See the paper by Richard Hemming and John A. Kay in this volume.

Because the start-up costs of administration and compliance are large relative to the additional costs generated when rates are increased, the switch to the value-added tax entailed fewer added collection costs for both the taxing authorities and the firms from which tax was collected than would have been the case in a nation with no comparable tax. Nevertheless, elaborate education and information programs accompanied the transition to the value-added tax in all these countries.

With the exception of Germany, the countries included in this volume have unitary governments; Germany alone allows the states, or *Länder,* to have significant independent power. In neither Germany nor, perforce, the other five nations did the value-added tax supplant important revenue sources of lower levels of government. In Germany part of the revenue from the value-added tax is distributed to the *Länder,* and, as Dieter Pohmer makes clear, the formula for this distribution has generated considerable controversy.[17]

The degree of compliance and the cost of administration seem to depend both on whether businesses are accustomed to keeping good written records and on the shares of activity carried out by small businesses. Compliance with the value-added tax in Italy is considerably poorer than it is in the other five countries. All nations have adopted rules exempting firms with low sales, although some nations allow these firms to elect to be subject to the value-added tax if it is in their interest. Some nations have special rules excluding farmers from the tax. In effect they pay no tax on sales and the loss of tax credits accrued on purchases is offset through a special deduction at the next stage in the production cycle. Because agricultural commodities typically are taxed, mostly at reduced rates, when sold by wholesalers or processors, the government does not suffer a loss of revenue.

Distribution of the Tax Burden

European experience with the value-added tax proves that it is possible to convert a tax that in its simplest form is proportional with respect to consumption and regressive with respect to income into a tax that is progressive with respect to consumption and proportional or slightly progressive with respect to income. The use of different rates for different classes of goods and services and of zero rating and exemptions is the mechanism for achieving this goal.

17. See the paper by Dieter Pohmer, pp. 99–100.

European experience does not, however, provide conclusive evidence that the goal should be sought. Participants at the conference agreed that the use of multiple rates and especially of exemptions complicates administration and compliance and distorts consumption in ways that are unlikely to promote economic efficiency. Most conference participants agreed that these disadvantages outweighed any gains from reduced regressivity. They held that distributional objectives should be sought with other instruments, notably income taxes and direct transfers. A few participants emphasized the incremental nature of political decisionmaking and argued that, whenever a decision is made, any undesirable distributional effects should be directly and immediately countered and not left for repair by some independent and separate action that might never be taken. The majority of conference participants felt that this view was needlessly compartmentalized and was productive of the kind of excessive rate variation that bedevils some European value-added taxes.

Special Problems

However simple the value-added tax may be in theory, European experience makes clear that it is not simple in practice. It creates a host of special problems that give rise to paperwork and more or less arbitrary distinctions. Whether the value-added tax is more or less encumbered by such stigmata than the personal or corporation income tax, the real property tax, or the retail sales tax is not the issue; the point is that while the value-added tax, compared with individualized taxes such as the personal income tax, is simple and cheap to administer, it is not the simple, self-enforcing tax that some of its less sophisticated advocates have suggested. Among the special problems of value-added taxation highlighted by European experience that would be important in the United States are the following. (Some of these problems are compounded if an attempt is made to tax different commodities at different rates.)

First, problems arise in the transition to a value-added tax whenever the revenue is used to replace a preexisting tax. For example, if the value-added tax replaced the corporation income tax, careful attention would have to be given to the depreciation allowed on investments undertaken near the point of transition and to the rules applicable under the value-added tax to the deduction of taxes paid on investment goods in order to avoid incentives to accelerate or to defer investment expenditures. Such problems arose in Europe because the value-added tax rules permitted credit for taxes paid on investment expenditures that were not allowed under the preexisting turnover tax; to avoid incentives for deferral of investment, several nations instituted temporary taxes on investment that are contrary to the spirit of the consumption type of value-added tax.

Adoption of the value-added tax (or of any other kind of taxation of current consumption) would raise a difficult transitional question of intergenerational equity. The retired of today worked most of their lives subject to the personal income and payroll taxes. To the extent that they are now financing consumption out of savings on which taxes have already been paid, they are not subject to additional income taxes. The introduction of a value-added tax, part of the proceeds of which are used to lower either personal income or payroll taxes, would place an added burden on the retired by requiring them to pay tax on consumption from income already taxed under the income and payroll taxes. Active workers would be compensated by reductions in income or payroll taxes.[18] If the value-added tax was large, this double taxation of the retired would generate pressure for special relief. The problem would not arise if the value-added tax was used to pay for new services for the retired or if retirement income consisted of pensions or other income (Keogh plans or capital gains on owned homes) that had fully or partially escaped income taxation.

Whether the value-added tax replaces a prior tax or supports added spending, transitional problems arise if housing is subject to tax. Housing services are exempt in all the countries covered in this book. New residential construction is subject in varying degrees to value-added tax. To that degree, introduction of the value-added tax raises the gross price of newly constructed housing relative to that of existing housing (unless sales of existing housing are subject to tax, in which case the proper base is unclear). The result is a windfall gain for owners of existing homes.

Second, most European nations surveyed in this book have adopted special rules for agriculture. These rules are motivated by political considerations and by the fact that farmers in some European countries tend not to keep sufficiently accurate records to support the collection procedures of the value-added tax. This problem would be less serious in the United States, where farmers are accustomed to filing personal income tax returns and some are now incorporated.

Third, nonprofit institutions would pose a number of choices. Not all produce taxable outputs (the Red Cross, for example); others produce

18. Pensioners would also be helped where, as in the United Kingdom, pensions are subject to tax.

outputs that could be taxed but that probably would not be (nonprofit hospitals, for example). But if nonprofit hospitals were not taxed, how should profit-making hospitals be treated? A similar problem would arise concerning the treatment of public and private universities and colleges; and if it was decided not to tax either, what then should be the treatment of secretarial and technical schools, special educational courses provided by corporations, and other related educational and training activities? The private nonprofit sector is far larger in the United States than in European nations and these problems would be correspondingly magnified.

Fourth, while secondhand goods sold privately are always exempt in Europe, rules vary for secondhand goods sold by dealers and auctioneers. A European Economic Community commission has recommended that, at least for costly goods, the tax should be imposed only on the dealers' margins. Nevertheless, in at least one country (Germany) the competition from person-to-person trade in secondhand goods puts business-to-person trade in the same goods (automobiles) at a serious competitive disadvantage.[19]

Fifth, the services of many financial institutions are provided at little or no cost to depositors or shareholders who permit the financial institution to make use of their funds. To that extent the profits of the financial institution come from investment income rather than fees or charges collected for services rendered. To some degree investment income is merely held by financial institutions acting in their fiduciary capacity for depositors and shareholders. It would be extraordinarily complex to determine the income of financial institutions on which value-added tax should be collected and to allocate tax on purchased inputs in the computation of credits. For this reason most of the countries exempt some or all financial institutions from value-added tax.

Still other difficulties in administration must be resolved in deciding whether a business purchase is intended for business or personal use; a

19. This problem arises because it is not possible as a practical matter under a consumption type of value-added tax to levy the tax on the flow of consumption services from consumer durable goods. If households paid value-added tax only on this service flow, no problem would arise; but in that event, consistent tax treatment would require that all owners of consumer durables be regarded as businesses that rent durable goods to themselves. The imputed rental proceeds would be taxable and the "business" would be entitled to a credit for taxes paid when the durable good was purchased. Clearly, this "logically correct" approach would impose unacceptable and difficult administrative burdens by requiring every homeowner to file a value-added tax return as a rental business on the home's estimated imputed income.

similar problem arises under the retail sales tax. The business expense account, the subject of so much controversy under the personal income tax, would create similar problems under the value-added tax. The French have adopted the most stringent attitude of the countries treated in this book, flatly disallowing credit for business purchases of automobiles and gasoline on the ground that no practical method exists for distinguishing business from personal use.

These problems drawn from European experience illustrate the types of decisions that the designers and administrators of a value-added tax would have to make in the United States. The fact is that such decisions are made in Europe, and all the participants in the Brookings conference agreed that the value-added tax works smoothly, in many cases more smoothly than its designers had anticipated. The one country where such a verdict of successful operation cannot be sustained is Italy. The estimated extent of evasion of the Italian value-added tax is very great. Although some skepticism about these estimates was expressed at the conference, even a much reduced estimate would still imply serious inequities and distortions attributable to the tax. The success of most countries in resolving issues such as these indicates that the value-added tax can and does work, but that it is not free of the kinds of close decisions and more or less arbitrary choices that make tax collectors always and everywhere the butt of ridicule and the object of wrath.

Economic Effects

The lessons from European experience about the economic effects of the value-added tax are few. The most clear-cut is that the regressivity of the value-added tax can be moderated or eliminated by differentiating rates and exemptions. This result is consistent with the findings of other studies.[20]

Because European value-added taxes replaced taxes yielding similar amounts of revenue and similarly distributed across industries, the introduction of the value-added tax produced few detectable effects on the price level. Subsequent increases in value-added tax rates contributed in some measure to inflation. Econometric models cited later in this book suggest that an increase of one percentage point in the value-added tax rate tended to raise prices directly by somewhat less than one percentage point. This result accords with expectations, even if monetary policy is

20. D. W. Adams, "The Distributive Effects of VAT in the United Kingdom, Ireland, Belgium, and Germany," *Three Banks Review*, no. 128 (December 1980), pp. 21–37.

accommodating, because not all consumption is taxed. There is some evidence that prices rose further because of a wage-price spiral. The treatment of the value-added tax in official index numbers, especially the consumer price index, might be an important issue were the tax to be adopted here. The simple solution would be to include the tax in the indexes; in other words, the prices used in the indexes would include the tax. But this approach would accentuate any continuing wage-price spiral. The alternative solution would be to include prices net of tax. This approach would make the consumer price index show changes in the prices of private, but not public, goods, and it also would avoid the anomaly of using a tax whose burdens can be automatically shifted to others through cost-of-living-adjustment clauses in wage contracts and would minimize the impact of the tax on the wage-price spiral.[21] The consequences of monetary policy designed to prevent any increase in prices cannot be directly estimated from studies reported later in this book, because no country pursued such a policy and none of the models—estimates from which are also reported in this book—were simulated on the basis of such a policy.

Evidence on other economic effects is almost entirely lacking. No evidence was presented that the introduction of the value-added tax materially affected investment or saving. The value-added tax became a central element in the process of international economic integration in which five of the six countries covered in this book are involved. Though much has been made of the possible salutary effects on the balance of payments from adopting the value-added tax, there is also no evidence that it had any material impact on the balance of trade in four of the five countries that belong to the European Economic Community or in Sweden, which is not part of the EEC. Only in Italy, where disallowance of the deductibility of the preexisting turnover tax by the EEC was threatening the competitiveness of Italian exports, did the value-added tax have a directly perceptible effect on foreign trade, and the reasons for this were related to Italy's special problems in complying with the directives of the Community.

Lessons for the United States

European experience with the value-added tax can guide debate in the United States about the desirability of adopting it in two distinct ways. First, there are important differences between the political conditions

21. The same considerations would not apply to other indexes, such as the personal consumption deflator.

Table 1. The Value-Added Tax in Selected European Countries

Country	Year of introduction	General rate			Value-added tax receipts as percent of total revenues			Value-added tax receipts as percent of GDP			Total revenues as percent of GDP		
		Year of introduction	1980	Percent increase	Year after introduction	1978	Percent increase	Year after introduction	1978	Percent increase	Year after introduction	1978	Percent increase
Members of the European Economic Community													
Denmark	1967	10	22	120	18.7	21.2	13	6.8	9.2	35	36.1	43.6	21
France	1968	16.7	17.6	5	26.8	21.6	−19	9.7	8.6	−11	36.3	39.7	9
Germany	1968	10	13	30	16.6	15.1	−9	5.6	5.7	2	33.9	37.8	12
Netherlands	1969	12	18	50	14.6	16.0	10	5.8	7.5	29	39.9	46.8	17
Luxembourg	1970	8	10	25	11.9	10.4	−13	4.1	5.2	27	34.3	49.9	45
Belgium	1971	16	16	0	19.4	17.6	−9	7.1	7.8	10	36.5	44.2	21
Ireland	1972	16.4	20	22	16.3	19.5	20	5.1	6.5	27	31.5	33.4	6
Italy	1973	12	14	17	17.3	14.2	−18	4.9	4.6	−6	28.3	32.6	15
United Kingdom	1973	10	15	50	8.9	9.0	1	3.1	3.1	0	35.5	34.4	−3
Nonmembers of the European Economic Community													
Sweden	1969	11.1	23.5	112	14.1	13.2	−6	4.2	7.0	67	41.0	53.5	30
Norway	1970	20	20	0	22.7	20.4	−10	9.6	9.6	0	42.4	46.9	11
Austria	1973	16	18	12	19.0	19.7	4	7.3	8.2	12	38.4	41.4	8

Sources: International Bureau of Fiscal Documentation, *Guides to European Taxation*, vol. 4: *Value-Added Taxes in Europe* (Amsterdam: IBFD, selected issues); and Organization for Economic Cooperation and Development, *Revenue Statistics of OECD Member Countries, 1965–1979* (Paris: OECD, 1980), pp. 43, 52.

under which the decision was made in European nations and those now prevailing in the United States. Understanding these differences is central to recognizing why the circumstances surrounding the adoption of the value-added tax in Europe are not replicated here.

Second, any country will encounter a large number of technical problems in adopting a new tax; the experiences and practices of European countries can save the United States from having to learn the lessons others have already mastered.

The Political Context

The most important lesson that Americans can learn from European experience with the value-added tax is how different the circumstances under which the six European nations made their decisions were from those in the United States. First, France, which pioneered the value-added tax, and three of the other countries surveyed here used the value-added tax to replace production or turnover taxes. This replacement was a clear improvement. The United States has never had a turnover tax or a production tax.

Second, the value-added tax became central to the economic integration of the European Economic Community. Except in France, which developed the tax, and Sweden, which has remained outside the EEC, the perceived need to coordinate the taxation of consumption among members of an economic union to facilitate border adjustments played an important part in the adoption of the value-added tax. No such situation, of course, exists for the United States.

Third, five of the six countries have unitary governments in which authorities below the central government have little power independent of the central government. But in neither West Germany nor the other five countries do local governments levy a tax on the same base as the value-added tax. In the United States, forty-five states impose retail sales taxes at different rates on much of the same consumption base that would be subject to a consumption type of value-added tax. Several European speakers stressed that the need for harmonizing consumption taxes was felt more strongly in Europe than it appears to be in the United States; the sales tax differentials widely tolerated and avoided by U.S. taxpayers would not be considered acceptable in Europe.

Fourth, the value-added tax in Europe was intended as a substitute for other taxes, but it has been associated with an increase in taxation. As shown in table 1, the proportion of gross domestic product absorbed by taxation in five of the six countries increased after the value-added tax was adopted. These statistics strongly suggest that the value-added tax was a handy instrument at a time when government expenditures were rising. The tax was introduced and its rates were increased as part of a process by which the role and scope of governmental activity increased. While the value-added tax might be used to reduce other taxes and as part of a program of fiscal retrenchment in the United States, it is important to recognize that the United States would be blazing a trail of fiscal forbearance not traversed by any of the countries covered in this book.

The Central Technical Lesson

The central technical lesson of European experience is that multiple rates can be used to eliminate the regressivity of the value-added tax, but that the penalties in administrative complexity, increased compliance costs, and distortions in consumption decisions have been high and probably unjustified. Most conference participants agreed with Sijbren Cnossen[22] that it would be preferable to use other taxes and transfer payments to alleviate the undesirable distributional consequences generated by a value-added tax imposed at uniform rates.

European experience reported at the conference suggests, however, that this advice may be a counsel of perfection. In varying degrees all European countries except Denmark employ differentiated rates, to pursue distributional objectives and make the distributional pattern of the value-added tax resemble that of taxes it replaced. In either case, no country treated in this book has followed the advice of the majority of the conference participants to do away with varied rates and to reduce the number of exemptions; all conferees thought that the United States would follow the European pattern of differentiated rates and exemptions if it adopted the value-added tax. None, for example, believed that Congress would be able to resist the pressure to impose lower than average rates of taxation on such necessities as food, housing, and medicines, although most participants agreed that it would be unfortunate if Congress deviated from uniform rates.[23]

22. See pp. 58–59, below.

23. Congressman Ullman's original proposal provided a reduced rate for food, medical care, and residential housing. The revised bill excluded them from tax by applying a zero rate to them.

The Real Debate

The value-added tax should not be regarded as a tax panacea or a simple surgical device for extracting revenue painlessly from the body politic. Rather, its desirability should be considered within the context of a larger debate on tax structure. For many years scholarly debates and practical political contests have proceeded on whether equity and efficiency would be better served by a personal income tax or a personal consumption tax; on whether the tax system should be progressive and, if so, how progressive; on whether the corporation income tax in combination with the personal income tax doubly taxes corporate source income; and on whether social security benefits should be financed by payroll taxes alone or in combination with other sources of revenue. These debates show no signs of reaching a conclusion or of ending.

The value-added tax enters into each of the debates. It is one of a variety of devices for increasing reliance on consumption taxation. Alternatively, the number of provisions in the personal income tax under which savings escape current taxation, such as the deferral of taxation on pension funds, individual retirement accounts, and Keogh plans, could be increased. In principle, the extension of such deferral arrangements could gradually convert the personal income tax into a graduated tax on income less savings. A similar result could be achieved directly by replacing the personal income tax with a graduated expenditure tax. The value-added tax is yet another device for relieving saving of taxation, but only if the proceeds of such a tax are used to reduce personal income tax rates, to increase exemptions, or otherwise to lower tax rates applicable to saved income. Use of the revenues from a value-added tax for other purposes—for example, to replace payroll taxes imposed to support social security—would have no such effect. The liberalization of tax deferral for savings or the adoption of a personal consumption tax would avoid the difficult political problems in federal-state fiscal relations that enactment of a value-added tax would create.

It has long been recognized that distortions attributable to taxation tend to increase roughly with the square of the rate of taxation.[24] For this reason, such "excess burdens"—the lost consumer welfare from taxation

24. See, for example, Arnold C. Harberger, "Taxation, Resource Allocation, and Welfare," in John F. Due, ed., *The Role of Direct and Indirect Taxes in the Federal Revenue System* (Princeton University Press for the National Bureau of Economic Research and the Brookings Institution, 1964), pp. 25–80.

that exceeds the value of services that can be purchased with the revenue collected—tend to be greater under progressive than under proportional taxes. All developed industrial nations use progressive taxes extensively, however, to transfer from recipients of low incomes to recipients of high incomes some of the tax burdens that would result under proportional taxation. Where the balance should be struck in this trade-off between equality and efficiency is a continuing debate. The papers presented in this volume make clear that the value-added tax may add to regressivity or reduce it, except in the upper income ranges, where all consumption taxes are regressive except those with highly progressive rates; the outcome depends on whether the revenue is used to cut taxes or to increase government expenditures and on how particular taxes or expenditures are changed.[25] As Richard Hemming and John Kay point out, the recent increase in the British value-added tax combined with reductions in the personal income tax actually increased the progressivity of the tax system for most British families by a small amount. (This shift ignores the large reduction in top bracket rates affecting only those with the highest incomes, for whom the shift brought substantial relief.) The opposite result could easily have been achieved if the changes in the personal income tax had been differently designed. Clearly, the proceeds from a value-added tax could be used to replace part of the corporation income tax (a regressive change), to finance expanded health insurance benefits for the poor (a progressive change), to replace part of the payroll tax (a mildly progressive change), or be put to any number of other uses.[26] These examples underscore the point that the distributional effects of the adoption of the value-added tax or of an increase in its rates cannot be judged apart from the other taxes or expenditure changes that accompany it.

25. Progressivity here refers to the graduation of average tax rates according to income. However, this measure does not incorporate the effects on incomes of tax avoidance. If one takes such effects into account, it is possible to think of tax substitutions that lead to higher effective progressivity with respect to income or consumption and lower marginal tax rates relative to average tax rates. See James Buchanan and Geoffrey Brennan, "Tax Reform without Tears," in Henry J. Aaron and Michael J. Boskin, eds., *The Economics of Taxation* (Brookings Institution, 1980), pp. 33–53.

26. In the absence of bequests, inheritances, and uncertainty, a proportional payroll tax and a proportional consumption tax both levied at the same rate may be shown to change consumption possibilities for taxpayers identically. The U.S. payroll tax, however, is proportional only up to an earnings maximum and is zero above that point. Furthermore, the introduction of a consumption tax would have very different effects on different age groups from those of the payroll tax.

JEAN-PIERRE BALLADUR
and ANTOINE COUTIÈRE

France

THE value-added tax appeared first in France in 1954, initially covering the industrial sector alone. Its adoption followed a variety of turnover and sales taxes, the first of which was enacted in 1920 and modified periodically thereafter. Not until 1979, however, was the base of the value-added tax extended to include nearly all commodities as part of the process of tax harmonization within the European Economic Community.

In 1979 the valued-added tax yielded 48 percent of the revenue of the French government, making it by far the largest French tax. By comparison, the personal income tax produced 20 percent of government revenue, the corporation income tax 10 percent, and the tax on petroleum products 8 percent.

This paper briefly recounts that evolutionary process. It then describes the structure of the French value-added tax, the administrative rules under which it is collected, the administrative organization, and the distribution of the burden of the tax by social classes, income and consumption brackets, and family composition. It also presents the results of simulations of a variety of economic effects performed on a newly developed econometric model.

History

In 1920 a gross turnover tax was introduced to replace a system of specific excise taxes. It soon became apparent that the new system led to the unsystematic accumulation of tax liabilities at each stage of production. Modifications in 1937 and 1948 were designed to ameliorate this problem. In 1954 a full-blown consumption type of value-added tax was applied to the industrial sector; under this tax, for the first time investment expenditures were fully deductible. At the same time separate taxes on services and distribution were imposed.

Successive amendments broadened the base (1968), abolished the local tax on services and extended the value-added tax to cover services (1968), and extended coverage to virtually all economic activities, including those of most of the liberal professions (1979).

The coverage of the value-added tax is not yet total because agriculture is treated in a special manner and some liberal professions and financial activities and the public sector remain exempt.[1] Except for the special treatment of agriculture, these exceptions from general coverage are minor.

Structure and Administration

In general, nonexempt firms must pay tax on all sales at one of four rates: a normal rate of 17.6 percent, an increased rate of 33.33 percent, a reduced rate of 7 percent, or a zero rate.[2] The increased rate is applied to luxuries, the reduced rate to necessities, and the zero rate to exports.[3] In fact, the distinction between luxuries and necessities is laced with inconsistencies, but the intent and overall pattern are clear; the intent is to inject some progressivity into the value-added tax through reduced rates on goods bought disproportionately by low-income groups and through increased rates on goods bought disproportionately by high-income

1. Lawyers are temporarily exempt; the medical and paramedical, teaching, cultural, artistic, and sporting professions are permanently exempt.

2. Before 1977 there were five or six rates: in addition to the zero rate on exports, the rates before 1968 were 6.38 percent, 11.11 percent, 25.00 percent (the normal rate), 29.87 percent, and 33.33 percent. Rates have been changed five times since then, most recently on January 1, 1977, when the present schedule came into effect. Except for eleven months during 1968, the increased rate has been 33.33 percent and the reduced rate has been 7.00 to 7.53 percent. The normal rate was 20.00 to 23.44 percent between November 1968 and January 1, 1977.

3. The 7 percent reduced rate is applicable to foods (except beverages other than water and milk), including candy, margarine, and vegetable fat; products used in agriculture; medicines; passenger transportation; nonpornographic entertainment; books; residential rents; and meals served on the job. The increased rate is applied to cameras, radios, recording equipment, automobiles and motorcycles, furs, jewelry, perfume, tobacco, and pornographic entertainment. Special reduced rates apply generally in Corsica and the French overseas departments.

groups, and to free exports completely from tax burden by the zero rate.[4] Taxable businesses are entitled to take deductions for tax paid on goods used in producing output unless the output is exempt from the value-added tax (for example, insurance, financial services, certain liberal professions) or the input is explicitly nondeductible. Taxes on fuels and passenger cars are not deductible even when purchased by businesses; similarly, taxes on housing provided by businesses for executives, on business entertainment, and on gifts are not deductible. Such deductions are disallowed because the danger of tax avoidance would be great if they were permitted. In each case, the line between private use and professional use is imprecise.

Imports are subject to tax as soon as they clear customs, and taxes on exports are fully rebated to ensure that imports and domestically produced goods will be treated the same and that exports will leave without any tax burden. This approach permits the government of each nation applying a similarly structured value-added tax to set rates autonomously without directly affecting trade among nations.[5]

A Value-Added Tax Framework

To illustrate the operation of the value-added tax, the framework shown in table 1 may prove helpful. The table represents sales and purchases by each of three industries to the other two and to households and the imports and exports of each industry. No industry is assumed to make taxable sales to itself, and no imports are assumed to be exported without first passing through a domestic industry.

If all transactions are taxed at the same rate, revenues are equal to the tax rate, t, multiplied by the sum of sales to households by each industry and of direct household imports.

If one of the industries produces only investment goods or only materials used by other industries, it will have no sales to households and no net tax will be collected on its output, because, in the end, all taxable outputs of such an industry will be deductible inputs of another industry or will be exports.

4. To illustrate the anomalies, books are taxed at reduced rates, records at the increased rate; pastry is taxed at the reduced rate, fruit juice at the normal rate; radios are taxed at the increased rate, television sets at the normal rate; alcoholic beverages are taxed at the normal rate, tobacco at the increased rate.

5. The results of the simulations described below suggest that there may be indirect effects on trade.

Table 1. A Value-Added Tax Framework[a]

Sales	*Purchases*				
	Industry 1	*Industry 2*	*Industry 3*	*Households*	*Foreigners (exports)*
Industry 1	0	S_{12}	S_{13}	S_{1H}	S_{1E}
Industry 2	S_{21}	0	S_{23}	S_{2H}	S_{2E}
Industry 3	S_{31}	S_{32}	0	S_{3H}	S_{3E}
Foreigners (imports)	S_{I1}	S_{I2}	S_{I3}	S_{IH}	0

a. S_{ij} = sales by i to j
i, j = 1, 2, 3 (industries)
I = imports
E = exports
H = households.

All taxable transactions are subject to the same rate of tax, t, except exports, which are zero rated.

Tax collections are as follows:

If all industries are taxable:

From industry 1: $t[(S_{12} + S_{13} + S_{1H}) - (S_{21} + S_{31} + S_{I1})]$

From industry 2: $t[(S_{21} + S_{23} + S_{2H}) - (S_{12} + S_{32} + S_{I2})]$

From industry 3: $t[(S_{31} + S_{32} + S_{3H}) - (S_{13} + S_{23} + S_{I3})]$

On imports: $t(S_{I1} + S_{I2} + S_{I3} + S_{IH})$

Net revenue = $t(S_{1H} + S_{2H} + S_{3H} + S_{IH})$

If industry 3 is exempt:

From industry 1: $t[(S_{12} + S_{13} + S_{1H}) - (S_{21} + S_{I1})]$

From industry 2: $t[(S_{21} + S_{23} + S_{2H}) - (S_{12} + S_{I2})]$

On imports: $t(S_{I1} + S_{I2} + S_{I3} + S_{IH})$

Net revenue = $t(S_{1H} + S_{2H} + S_{IH} + S_{13} + S_{23} + S_{I3})$

The difference in revenue attributable to the exemption is:

$t(S_{13} + S_{23} + S_{I3} - S_{3H})$.

If one of the industries, say, industry 3, is exempt, then the government will lose revenues on sales by industry 3 to households (S_{3H}), but it will gain revenues on disallowed deductions on sales by industries 1 and 2 to industry 3 and on imports by industry 3. Exemptions reduce revenues because S_{3H} is greater than $(S_{13} + S_{23} + S_{I3})$; if purchases of industry 3 are taxed at higher rates than sales, revenues may actually decline.

This framework can be generalized to any number of rates and to any number of industries.[6]

6. In that event, revenue equals $(S_{ij})\ t - t'\ (S_{ij})$, where (S_{ij}) is an $n+1$ dimensional matrix of sales by industry i to industry j, the $n + 1$ row is imports, and the $n + 1$ column is exports; t is a column vector of the tax applied to industry j; t' is the transpose. If an industry produces different products subject to different tax rates, each tax rate group must be treated as a different "industry."

The Special Case of Agriculture

Farmers are treated in a manner analogous to exemption. They are not required to pay value-added tax nor are they entitled to itemize deductions for taxes paid on the products they buy. Instead, they are authorized to receive a payment from the government equal to a stipulated fraction, currently 3.5 percent for eggs and meats and 2.4 percent for other products, of their gross sales to businesses that are liable for value-added tax payments. Farmers are subject to the value-added tax for their compulsorily taxable activities.

Administration for Nonagricultural Enterprises

The value-added tax on nonagricultural enterprises is collected under one of three systems. Nonagricultural firms whose sales of goods are less than 500,000 francs (or whose sales of services are less than 150,000 francs) pay a lump-sum tax, set once every two years by the General Taxation Division, from which the value-added tax on purchases is subtracted.

Firms with sales up to twice the limit are subject to a simplified real turnover system under which returns are filed once a year, but taxpayers must declare turnover and make payments on account once a month unless liability is less than 500 francs, in which case quarterly declarations suffice.

The standard real turnover system applied to taxpayers with a sufficient volume of sales has more exacting rules. Bookkeeping must make it possible to distinguish taxable from exempt transactions, and to separate transactions subject to different rates into appropriate categories. Invoices must contain information on the value-added tax rate, the price of the commodity or service exclusive of tax, the amount of tax, and identification of the customer.

Of the 1,990,000 nonagricultural businesses subject to value-added tax in 1979, 1,015,000 (51 percent) came under the lump-sum system; 401,000 (20 percent) came under the simplified real turnover system; and 574,000 (29 percent) came under the standard real turnover system. However, 89 percent of all revenues collected came from businesses subject to the real turnover system.

Small businesses also receive tax relief. Value-added tax liabilities of less than 1,350 francs a year, disregarding deductions for investments, are waived. Liabilities that fall between 1,350 and 5,400 francs are re-

Table 2. Distribution of Tax Collection, by Sector

Sector	*Percent of total revenue*
Households	72.1
Firms	17.3
General government	9.8
Financial institutions	0.8
Total	100.0

Source: Bureau des Etudes Fiscales, Direction de la Prévision, "VAT 79 Model," *Statistiques et Etudes Financières*, Série Orangé (Ministère de l'Economie, forthcoming, 1981).

duced by one-third of the difference between the liability and 5,400 francs. Craftsmen receive additional relief.

Two divisions of the Ministry of Budget, the General Taxation Division and the General Customs Division, share responsibility for collecting and enforcing the value-added tax.[7] The former is responsible for collecting the value-added tax on all domestic transactions; 11,500 employees are involved in this activity. The latter handles the collection of the value-added tax on imports and on gasoline.

Effects of the Tax

In theory, the consumption-type value-added tax falls only on consumption. In practice, more than one-quarter of the value-added tax is collected from businesses, financial institutions, and the government (see table 2). This deviation of practice from theory is attributable in part to the existence of exemptions and in part to the nondeductibility of certain outlays, notably automobiles and gasoline. These taxes, which are not offset against the collections of some firm that sells to final purchasers or abroad, eventually burden the owner of such businesses, other factors of production, or consumers. The truth is that these burdens are not related to consumption in the simple way that value-added taxes are thought to be.

Distribution

The National Institute of Statistics and Economic Studies has carried out a number of surveys of household consumption on the basis of which

7. Direction Générale des Impôts and Direction Générale des Douanes, respectively.

Table 3. Value-Added Tax Burden as Percent of Consumption, by Social Class and Consumption Level, 1969

Description	Tax as percent of consumption
Social class	
Farmers	9.4
Farm workers	10.6
Independent professionals	
All	11.9
Learned professions and industrialists	12.4
Senior executives	11.7
Managerial staff	
All	11.8
Foremen	11.4
White-collar workers	11.6
Blue-collar workers	11.3
Inactive population	11.1
All classes	11.3
Consumption level (francs)	
2,000–3,000	10.5
3,000–4,000	10.7
4,000–5,000	10.7
5,000–6,000	11.0
6,000–8,000	11.0
8,000–10,000	11.3
10,000–15,000	11.7
Over 15,000	11.9
All levels	11.3

Source: C. Begin and J. Delpech, "TVA et Consommation des Ménages," in *Statistiques et Etudes Financières*, Série Orangé, no. 12 (Ministère de l'Economie, 1973).

the distribution of value-added tax burdens can be estimated. The results of these estimates are reported in tables 3 and 4. The estimates distribute value-added tax burdens based on consumption patterns and the estimated rate of taxation on each category of consumer goods.

There is little variation in the value-added tax burden by social class (see table 3). The burden on farmers and farm workers is somewhat below average and that on industrialists and professionals somewhat above average. Otherwise, deviations from the average are small. There is likewise little variation in the value-added tax burden by consumption class, although a slight degree of progressivity with respect to consumption is discernible. Data not reported here indicate that there is little variation in the burdens of employees on the basis of family status. Couples with

Table 4. Value-Added and Income Tax Burdens, by Income Bracket, 1972

Income bracket (francs)	*Number of households (millions)*	*Average income (francs)*	*Average income tax (francs)*	*Average value-added tax (francs)*	*Average tax rates (percent)*		
					Income	*Value-added*	*Total*
Under 10,000	2.8	5,255	12	1,165	0.23	22.17	22.40
10,000–15,000	1.9	12,260	166	1,885	1.35	15.38	16.73
15,000–20,000	2.0	17,108	403	1,986	2.36	11.61	13.97
20,000–30,000	3.6	24,139	850	2,834	3.52	11.74	15.26
30,000–50,000	3.6	37,286	2,353	3,769	6.31	10.11	16.42
50,000–75,000	1.3	58,231	5,780	5,070	9.93	8.71	18.64
75,000–100,000	0.4	83,643	11,287	6,636	13.49	7.93	21.42
Over 100,000	0.3	163,480	34,152	8,886	20.89	5.44	26.33
Total or average	15.9	28,663	2,370	2,893	8.27	10.09	18.36

Source: Authors' estimates.

no children pay 12 percent of income in value-added tax; couples with three children pay 11.1 percent.

The value-added tax is highly regressive with respect to total income (see table 4).[8] In fact, the uniformly progressive French personal income tax combines with the value-added tax to produce a U-shaped distribution of the burden, first falling as income rises and then rising again. The distributional pattern of the value-added tax with respect to income is sharply different from that with respect to consumption. The tax is regressive with respect to the former and proportional or slightly progressive with respect to the latter; the reason for this discrepancy is that the fraction of income consumed declines sharply as income rises.

Prices and Government Revenue

Tax policy has pervasive effects on the economy, influencing real economic activity, prices, wages, and foreign trade. To encompass all of these effects systematically requires a fully articulated econometric model. This section reports the results of using such a model to analyze the conse-

8. In fact, regressivity may be exaggerated in table 4. Underreporting of income to avoid *income* tax is greater than underreporting of consumption, on which value-added tax estimates are based.

quences of decreasing the value-added tax alone or in combination with compensating increases in other revenues.

This analysis rests on two models: the VAT 79 model, which shows the change in revenues resulting from changes in value-added tax rates, exemptions, and other provisions;[9] and the METRIC model, which is used primarily for short-run economic forecasting and for analyzing the short-run effects of changes in policies.[10]

A reduction in the value-added tax rate of one percentage point would reduce consumer prices by 0.7 percentage point. Prices of food and industrial products would fall 0.8 percentage point, those of transportation and telecommunications 0.6 percentage point, and those of services 0.4 percentage point, a pattern that reflects the incomplete coverage of services. The price of investment goods would fall by 0.25 percentage point, largely because of the nondeductibility of tax on purchases of automobiles. Revenues in 1980 would fall by 16 billion francs, or 6.6 percent of value-added tax revenues.

Based on the METRIC model, a reduction in the value-added tax rate of two percentage points would have the effects shown in table 5 if the monetary authorities pursued a policy of holding interest rates constant. The immediate effect of the policy shift is an increase in real disposable income because prices drop. As a result, final demands increase for both domestic and imported products. After three years, export prices have declined because decreasing consumer prices reduce wage increases, but the balance of trade continues to be negatively influenced. The government deficit arising from the tax cut is always smaller than the direct revenue loss because of induced increases in economic activity, and becomes quite small with time.

9. The VAT 79 model is a collection of six input-output tables, one for each of the four legal rates (three since 1979), exempt activities, and zero rates. On an industry-by-industry basis it shows the value of sales to and from each of 600 industry-commodity groups. These six tables are aggregated to show the consequences of various changes in revenue in the aggregate and by industry. Bureau des Etudes Fiscales, Direction de la Prévision, "VAT 79 Model," *Statistiques et Etudes Financières,* Série Orangé (Ministère de l'Economie, forthcoming, 1981).

10. The METRIC model is a quarterly model consisting of 886 equations and 350 exogenous variables. It is an eclectic model incorporating hypotheses that have been supported by analysis in France and other countries. It places considerable emphasis on capacity limitations and disequilibria. A full description of an earlier version of this model may be found in "Le Modèle METRIC," in *Annales de l'INSEE,* nos. 26–27 (April–September 1977).

Table 5. Effects on Selected Economic Variables after One, Three, and Five Years of a Two Percentage Point Reduction in Value-Added Tax Rates, Based on the VAT 79 and METRIC Models

Variable	*After one year*	*After three years*	*After five years*
Real quantities			
Gross national product	0.6	0.9	1.2
Household consumption	0.8	0.9	1.1
Investment	2.1	1.1	1.4
Imports	0.8	0.6	0.7
Exports	−0.1	0.3	0.7
Prices			
Household consumption	−1.6	−2.3	−2.9
Investment	−0.9	−1.5	−2.3
Exports	−0.2	−0.6	−1.0
Other			
Wage rate	−1.5	−1.9	−2.1
Employment	0.2	0.6	0.9
Disposable income	−1.0	−1.3	−1.6
Government deficit	−10.0	−8.8	−6.1
Money supply	−0.4	−1.0	−1.3

Source: Authors' estimates.

Table 6 contains similar estimates for the same reduction in value-added tax rates matched by an increase in wage taxes paid by employees or by employers that is sufficient to hold the government deficit constant during the first year. Either approach causes domestic prices to fall, but the replacement of two percentage points of value-added tax with the employer wage tax is associated with an increase in real output, while the replacement with a wage tax on employees leads to a reduction in real output for at least three years. In contrast, the trade balance improves if the wage tax on employees is increased, but deteriorates if the wage tax on employers is increased; this difference is explained by the difference in the direct imports by households and in the direct impact of the tax switches on producer prices.

Conclusion

In our judgment, the meaning of the French experience for the United States is limited because of specific features of the French economy.

First, the value-added tax should be a national tax, not a state or local

Table 6. Effects on Selected Economic Variables after One, Three, and Five Years of a Two Percentage Point Reduction in Value-Added Tax Rates and a Compensating Increase in Wage Taxes on Employees or Employers, Based on the VAT 79 and METRIC Models

	After one year		*After three years*		*After five years*	
Variable	*Employee wage tax*	*Employer wage tax*	*Employee wage tax*	*Employer wage tax*	*Employee wage tax*	*Employer wage tax*
Real quantities						
Gross national product	−0.1	0.5	−0.1	0.5	0.3	0.6
Household consumption	0.0	0.8	−0.4	0.6	−0.2	0.7
Investment	−0.4	1.1	−0.8	0.3	0.7	0.5
Imports	−0.4	0.7	−0.5	0.4	−0.1	0.5
Exports	0.1	−0.1	0.4	0.1	0.8	0.1
Prices						
Household consumption	−1.5	−1.4	−2.2	−1.5	−2.9	−1.6
Investment	−0.8	−0.6	−1.4	−0.8	−2.0	−0.9
Exports	−0.2	0.0	−0.7	−0.1	−1.1	−0.2
Other						
Wage rate	−1.4	−1.3	−2.0	−1.3	−2.4	−1.3
Employment	0.0	0.2	0.0	0.3	0.3	0.4
Disposable income	−1.9	−0.8	−2.4	−0.8	−2.8	−0.8
Government deficit	1.0	−1.2	−2.7	−0.2	1.9	−0.4
Money supply	−1.0	−0.5	−1.7	−0.8	−1.9	−0.8

Source: Authors' estimates.

tax (even if the rates were identical among the states). To raise local revenues, it would be better to impose a nondeductible tax on retail sales.

Second, the full effects of the value-added tax strongly depend both on the economic situation at the time the tax is introduced and on which taxes the value-added tax replaces.

Third, we do not recommend rate differentiation. Though administration is not complicated, such differentiation is an inefficient way to achieve redistributive objectives. Even if many commodities were zero rated, significant progressivity could not be obtained.

ANTONIO PEDONE

Italy

THE value-added tax began in Italy in 1973, six years after directives of the European Economic Community called on all members to adopt the tax and three years after the deadline set for its adoption. Since its adoption, the Italian parliament has enacted more than seventy laws applying to it, and more than eighty ministerial decrees have been handed down. It is therefore much too early to measure the ultimate effects of the present value-added tax law on the Italian economy.

This paper describes the process by which the value-added tax was adopted in Italy, outlines the special features of the tax as enacted, and emphasizes the problem of tax evasion that has plagued its administration. It then turns to the effects of the tax on prices, investment, international trade, and income distribution; none of these effects are known with certainty both because continuing legislative change maintains a perennial state of incomplete adjustment and because the full effects of evasion, by its very nature, are difficult to specify.

Adoption of the Tax

Enactment of the value-added tax in Italy took so long in part because it replaced a large number of other taxes, in part because other major tax changes accompanied its adoption, and in part because the parliament chose an unusually complex tax structure.

The value-added tax replaced a multistage turnover tax, the *imposta generale sull'entrata,* many excise taxes levied at the municipal and national level, stamp taxes, and other minor indirect taxes. Of these, the turnover tax was by far the most important, but it suffered from well-known failings. It is impossible to know exactly how much of the price of any commodity is tax, because the exact amount of tax depends on how many stages the commodity has passed through during production. For a similar reason, the turnover tax encourages vertical integration, thereby eliminating transfers between stages of production, even when other economic considerations do not justify integration.[1] The difficulty of measuring how much of the final value of commodities was represented by taxes made it impossible accurately to provide the rebates on exports required in the European Economic Community. Because such rebates were calculated on an average basis, they inevitably provided some exporters, especially those that were vertically integrated, with hidden subsidies, and provided some domestic producers with some degree of protection. For these reasons, the turnover tax was an obstacle to European economic integration. Furthermore, the value-added tax was expected to encourage investment more than the turnover tax had, because investment goods are exempt under the former but were subject to tax under the latter.[2]

Although the government initially declared its intent to adopt the value-added tax without delay, passive and active opposition came from many sources. Tax administrators pointed out the administrative problems of collecting tax from retailers, the higher cost of collecting the value-added tax than of collecting the taxes it would replace, and the increased opportunities for evasion. Trade unions feared that the tax would be regressive and urged below-average rates on necessities. Exporters opposed the tax because they feared that rebates would be smaller than those allowed under the turnover tax; this opposition weakened only after the Commission of the European Economic Community required the Italian government to reduce such rebates. Business in general and small business in particular opposed the tax, concerned about the costs of added

1. The importance of this incentive has been exaggerated, and it is doubtful whether it alone was sufficient to induce integration; on the other hand, there can be no doubt that the turnover tax favors vertically integrated firms. The savings from *full* integration could not exceed 2 to 3 percent of the final price. See Antonio Pedone, *Il sistema tributario e la concentrazione industriale* (The Tax System and Industrial Concentration) (Milan: Giuffré, 1972), p. 79.

2. A detailed list of the advantages and disadvantages of the value-added tax as perceived by Italian writers at the time of its adoption is contained in C. Cosciani, *L'imposta sul valore aggiunto* (The Value-Added Tax) (Rome: Ricerche, 1968); Francesco Forte, *Le imposte sulle vendite e sul valore aggiunto* (Sales Taxes and Value-Added Taxes) (Turin: Einaudi, 1973); and Franco Reviglio, *Lezioni sulla riforma tributaria* (Lectures on Tax Reform) (Turin: Giappichelli, 1974).

record-keeping that the new tax would require. As two observers noted, "Each interest had its own reasons for opposing the new tax; indeed each had different reasons. But each complemented every other one in presenting an already weak and faltering Italian Government with strong imperatives against innovative action."[3]

In the end, the Italian government twice sought and received a deferral in meeting the January 1970 deadline set by the EEC directives for adoption of the value-added tax by all members; the first postponement was until January 1972, the second until July 1972, and the actual date of introduction was January 1973. Not until April 1979 did Italy bring its value-added tax fully into compliance with the sixth directive of the EEC issued in 1977. These delays seriously hinder efforts to identify the economic effects of the introduction of the tax. Producers, investors, and consumers all had lengthy periods during which they could alter their behavior in response to the anticipated tax. The effects observable at the time of adoption are only part of the story.

Changes in the remainder of the tax structure and in relations between the central government and the municipalities either accompanied or quickly followed the introduction of the value-added tax. A municipal sales tax was repealed, local finance was reformed, and two new income taxes, one on individuals and one on corporations, replaced previously existing schedular income taxes.

These changes increased tax collections as a fraction of gross domestic product only slightly but boosted the share of direct taxes considerably (see table 1). This increase occurred because the new income taxes rise more than proportionately when income increases. The striking aspect of table 1 is the failure of value-added tax collections to increase as a fraction of gross domestic product despite periodic increases in rates.

Administration

Administration of the value-added tax is burdened in Italy by the unusually complex structure of the tax. The tax has been imposed at as many as nine different rates and never fewer than four; currently it is imposed at five different rates—2, 8, 15 (the "normal" rate), 18, and 35

3. Donald J. Puchala and Carl F. Lankowski, "The Politics of Fiscal Harmonization in the European Communities," *Journal of Common Market Studies,* vol. 15 (March 1977), pp. 155–79.

Table 1. General Government Tax Collections, Total and by Category, as a Percentage of Gross Domestic Product, Selected Years, 1960–79

Year	*Total revenue*	*Direct taxes*	*Social security contributions*	*Value-added tax*	*Other indirect taxes*	*Total indirect taxes*
1960	27.6	5.7	8.9	...	13.0	13.0
1965	29.3	6.6	10.4	...	12.3	12.3
1970	29.7	6.0	11.6	...	12.1	12.1
1973	28.4	6.0	12.6	4.5	5.3	9.8
1974	28.6	6.0	12.8	4.5	5.3	9.8
1975	29.4	6.7	14.0	4.0	4.7	8.7
1976	31.4	7.8	14.0	4.5	5.1	9.6
1977	32.7	8.7	13.8	4.9	5.3	10.2
1978	34.4	10.1	14.2	4.9	5.3	10.2
1979	33.8	9.8	14.5	4.4	5.1	9.5

Source: *Relazione generale sulla situazione economica del paese* (Annual Economic Report), Rome, selected years.

percent.[4] Transactions may be taxable, excluded, exempt, or nontaxable (zero rated). Zero-rated transactions include all exports, international transportation, and many transactions of enterprises engaged in international operations. Refunds of taxes on inputs are paid on zero-rated transactions. No refund of taxes paid on purchased inputs may be claimed on excluded and exempt transactions. Even if a firm produces both taxable and excluded products, it may deduct all value-added tax paid on inputs. However, no deductions for tax paid on inputs may be claimed against exempt transactions; for exempt transactions all tax paid on purchased inputs must be wholly passed on or absorbed, as no other tax liability against which to offset it is allowed. To complicate matters further, firms may engage in all four classes of transactions during any tax period. Furthermore, the rules governing the degree to which tax paid on previous stages of production may be offset against the tax liability of the firm have been amended periodically, most recently in April 1979. Finally, particular sectors of the economy enjoy special treatment. Small

4. Rates were initially set at 1, 6, 12, and 18 percent on January 1, 1973; the normal rate was 12 percent; on July 9, 1974, a 30 percent rate for some commodities was added. On June 24, 1975, a 6 percent rate was added. On March 18, 1976, a 9 percent rate was added. On February 8, 1977, 12 and 35 percent rates were added, and the normal rate was boosted to 14 percent. On July 3, 1980, the present rate structure came into effect.

farmers, for example, sell their goods, applying to their sales the special reduced rate applicable to agricultural products. They may choose to retain the taxes thus collected, in which case they lose the right to claim credit for taxes paid by their suppliers, or they may pay the tax and claim the credit.

The taxing authorities annually receive 3.6 million returns. Firms with total sales exceeding 480 million lire a year must follow specified rules for invoicing, records, and reporting. Firms with gross sales below 480 million lire and a special group of taxpayers, including all retail stores, artists, professionals, and artisans, are subject to more relaxed requirements. This group is required only to keep a record of sales, and the deduction for value-added tax paid on inputs is set equal to a given percentage of taxable sales—70 percent for retail stores, 20 percent for artists and professionals, and 50 percent for artisans. This *forfait* system reduces the costs of administration and of verification of the liability of taxpayers who keep notoriously inadequate records, but it is subject to abuse and is one of the main causes of evasion.

Reliable estimates of the extent of evasion are difficult to make. Table 2 indirectly reports estimates of evasion for 1977. The table shows the value added by sector estimated from the national income accounts and actually reported on value-added tax returns. The difference is a measure of value added not reported on tax returns. The precision of the estimates is open to question. To the extent that the national income accounts understate Italian value added, the estimates of evasion are too low. To the extent that people neglect to report exempt or lightly taxed transactions, the estimates may overstate revenue loss. Under any plausible interpretation, however, evasion is pervasive and large, reducing value-added tax collections by as much as two-thirds in some broad sectors and by two-fifths overall. Only in the production of energy, which is a quasi-public enterprise, and in manufacturing, which is dominated by large firms that require modern accounting procedures and complete records to do business, is evasion below 40 percent.

To reduce evasion, the government has required some changes in administrative procedures. Beginning in 1979 goods in transit have had to be accompanied by tax certificates. Since March 1980 hotels and restaurants have had to issue tax receipts for most of their services and must retain one copy themselves. Whether these procedures will succeed in curbing evasion remains an open question.

Table 2. Estimates of Value Added from the National Income Accounts and Amounts Reported on Value-Added Tax Returns, by Sector, 1977

	National accounts[a]		*Value-added tax returns*		*Difference*		*Difference as percent of national accounts estimate*
Economic sector	*Trillions of lire*	*Percent*	*Trillions of lire*	*Percent*	*Trillions of lire*	*Percent*	
Energy production	6.3	5.7	6.3	9.5	0.0	0.0	0.0
Manufacturing	47.9	43.6	35.6	53.5	12.4	28.1	25.9
Construction	14.0	12.8	6.1	9.2	7.9	17.9	56.4
Trade	21.4	19.5	7.6	11.4	13.9	31.5	64.9
Hotels and restaurants	4.1	3.7	1.9	2.8	2.8	6.3	68.3
Transportation (excluding public transportation)	4.8	4.3	2.7	4.1	2.0	4.5	41.7
Other services	11.4	10.4	6.3	9.5	5.1	11.7	44.7
Total	109.9	100.0	66.5	100.0	44.1	100.0	40.1

Source: Estimates by G. Campa, based on data from Ministero delle Finanze (Ministry of Finance).
a. Output at market prices, less gross fixed investment and value-added tax on imports.

Economic Effects

As noted earlier, the economic effects of the value-added tax are hard to identify empirically, in part because of the long delay between the announcement and the introduction of the tax. Nevertheless, some analyses of these effects have been made.

Price Effects

Because the value-added tax replaced the turnover tax and the yields of the two taxes were similar,[5] it would seem that the effect on prices of removing one tax should just offset the effects of introducing the other. The distribution of the two taxes was not identical, however, and there was some fear that the prices of goods on which the tax burdens were reduced would not fall or would fall by less than the prices of goods on which the tax liability rose. Furthermore, the shift of taxes from investment to consumption goods could be expected to boost consumer prices even if they left broader indexes unchanged. All of these analyses presumed that changes in turnover and value-added taxes would affect commodity prices rather than factor prices.

A number of studies documented the fact that the switch in taxes would affect different industries differently.[6] Only the adoption of a multiple-rate value-added tax would prevent large increases in the tax burden on goods regarded as "basic" or as "necessities." Conversely, the results showed that the tax burden on investment goods and exports would drop

5. During the last year of operation (1972), the turnover tax yielded 2,212 million lire; during the first full year of operation (1973), the value-added tax yielded 2,484 million lire. See *Relazione generale sulla situazione economica del paese 1975* (Annual Economic Report for 1975), pp. 454–55.

6. Some studies used national income accounts data. See, among others, Emilio Gerelli and Gianni Sartorati, *Contributo alla riforma tributaria* (A Contribution to Tax Reform) (Milan: ILSES, 1964); Mario Rey, *Alcuni elementi quantitative per l'applicazione in Italia di un'imposta sul valore aggiunto* (Some Quantitative Aspects of the Adoption of a Value-Added Tax in Italy) (Naples: Studi Economici, 1965); and V. Visco, "Calcolo dell'aliquota di un'imposta sul valore aggiunto" (Estimated Share of the Value-Added Tax), in *Studi sull'imposta sul valore aggiunto* (A Study on the Value-Added Tax Rate) (Milan: Giuffré, 1968), pp. 129–61. Other studies used input-output tables. See, among others, Alberto Cassone, Mario Locascio, and Franco Reviglio, "Gli effetti dell'IVA sui carichi impositivi intersettoriali" (VAT Effects on the Intersectoral Tax Burden), *Mondo Economico,* vol. 12 (November 1972), pp. 26–32; Filippo Cavazzuti and Carlo D'Adda, "Imposta sul valore aggiunto e prezzi: un'applicazione dello schema input-output" (VAT and Prices in the Input-Output Table), *Note Economiche,* vol. 2 (December 1972), pp. 176–87.

sharply. Studies such as these contributed to the decision to have a large number of separate rates in order to achieve "neutrality," in other words, to preserve existing patterns of tax liability.

At the aggregate level, most estimates of the average increase in prices ranged from 2 to 6 percent, given a value-added tax of 10 percent. These estimates differed according to the assumption made about how firms would change their prices in response to changes in their tax liabilities, which in turn depended on assumptions made about the degree of monopoly power they enjoyed, external economic conditions, and fiscal and monetary policies. It is impossible to assess the validity of these forecasts, not only because of the numerous alternative assumptions used, but also because the value-added tax adopted was different from the one used in the simulations, because the effects of the tax were in some degree anticipated well before its introduction, and because shortly after its adoption price controls were introduced and the oil crisis occurred.

Despite uncertainties about past price effects, payroll taxes were cut by 1.4 trillion lire in 1977 and were replaced by the value-added tax to reduce both inflation and export prices. Such a change would have no impact on inflation if money wages and markups were unaffected. In that event, the value-added tax would simply replace the payroll tax as a deduction from the gross receipts of employers on the average; while some redistribution in taxes among employers might occur, there would be no aggregate effect on prices.[7] However, some anti-inflationary effect would result from the switch if markups by employers were based on money costs of production exclusive of the value-added tax and if the markup percentage was not increased sufficiently when payroll taxes were cut to offset the decrease in the base to which the markup percentage was applied. In that event, the reduction of payroll taxes would cause employers to lower their markup amounts, thus cutting inflation.[8]

7. This argument is made by Franco Modigliani and Tommaso Padoa-Schioppa, "La politica economica in una economia con salari indicizzati al 100% e piu" (Economic Policy in an Economy with Wage Indexation of 100 Percent and More), *Moneta e Credito,* vol. 30 (March 1977) pp. 3–53.

8. This argument is advanced by Antonio Pedone, "L'inflazione in Italia: tendenze e previsione" (Inflation in Italy: Trends and Forecasts), in *La lotta al'inflazione* (The Fight against Inflation) (Rome: Editori Riuniti, 1977), pp. 47–70; Alessandro Roncaglia, Mario Tonveronachi, Carlo Cararosa, and Marco Crivellini, "Commenti a un recente studio di Modigliani e Padoa-Schioppa" (Comments on a Recent Study by Modigliani and Padoa-Schioppa), *Moneta e Credito,* vol. 31 (March 1978), pp. 3–50; and Ruggero Paladini, "Sulla fiscalizazione degli oneri sociali" (On the Substitution of Social Security Contributions by Taxes), *Note Economiche,* vol. 8 (September 1978), pp. 121–26.

While the debate about the impact on prices of replacing part of payroll taxes with value-added taxes remains unsettled, the effect of the switch on export prices is not in question. Unless domestic prices of exportable goods increased by the full amount of the value-added tax, export prices would decrease.

Empirical estimates support the proposition that the replacement of the payroll tax by the value-added tax has reduced not only export prices but domestic inflation as well. One study published by the Bank of Italy concluded that the 1.4 trillion lire cut in payroll taxes lowered the rate of increase in unit production costs in manufacturing by four percentage points.[9] Another study based on the 1974 input-output table concluded that a reduction in payroll taxes of one trillion lire and an equal increase in value-added taxes would eventually reduce export prices of manufactured goods by 3.5 percent and the general price level by 2 percent; these estimates take account of the effect on money wages of indexing formulas and assume that firms hold unit profits constant in money terms.[10] If firms increase their profits to fully offset the cut in payroll taxes, there is no initial effect on export prices, and in the end they increase by 1 percent and consumer prices by almost 2 percent.

Investment

The impact of the value-added tax on investment received wide consideration when the tax was adopted. Because investment was taxed under the turnover tax but was to be exempt under the value-added tax, the government was concerned that business would defer investment during the transitional period. To prevent this effect, the government allowed firms to deduct investments made after 1971 from the base for the turnover tax. Deductions also were allowed for additions to inventories. Although the switch to the value-added tax provided some industries with substantial benefits and removed the tax on investment, there is no evidence that investment increased.

International Trade

The introduction of the value-added tax may have improved the balance of trade or the exchange rate slightly for two reasons special to Italy. First, the Commission of the European Economic Community had already

9. Banca d'Italia, *Relazione, 1977* (Rome: Bank of Italy, 1978), p. 129.

10. Vieri Ceriani, *Effetti sui prezzi del prelievo per imposte indicrette, contribuit sociali e tariffe* (Effects on Prices of Indirect Taxes, Social Security Contributions, and Public Utility Charges) (Bank of Italy, Research Department, 1980).

Table 3. Sources of Value-Added Tax, 1973–79
Billions of lire

Year	*Domestic transactions*	*Imports*	*State monopolies*	*Gross tax*	*Rebates*	*Net tax*
1973	2,267	1,542	192	4,001	0	4,001
1974	2,076	2,763	220	5,059	0	5,059
1975	2,733	2,619	258	5,610	1,100	4,510
1976	4,025	3,819	295	8,139	1,356	6,783
1977	5,339	5,056	344	10,739	1,357	9,382
1978	6,715	5,771	400	12,886	1,924	10,962
1979	7,638	7,537	466	15,641	3,150	12,491

Source: Ministero delle Finanze (Ministry of Finance), *Entrate Tributarie Erariali* (Central Government Tax Revenues) Rome, selected monthly issues.

reduced the rebates payable on exports on account of the turnover tax. Second, the effective rate of taxation on imports is higher than that on domestically produced, import-competing goods because evasion on imports is much more difficult than it is on domestically produced goods. The amount of value-added tax on imports has increased faster than that on domestic transactions (see table 3); the two amounts were about equal in 1979. It should also be noted that the proportion of gross value-added tax receipts rebated on exports increased from 13 percent in 1977 to 20 percent in 1979.

Distribution

The effect of the value-added tax on the distribution of tax burdens was the most hotly debated issue when the tax was under consideration. It was feared that the new tax would offset the slight degree of progressivity in the income tax. This fear led to below-average rates for commodities consumed or produced disproportionately by people of modest income—the products of agriculture and small business.

On balance, the effort to make the value-added tax somewhat progressive seems to have succeeded. One study, based on the rates put into effect in 1973, found that the value-added tax rose from 5 percent of family expenditure among the lowest economic classes to 9.7 percent among the highest class and that variation in rates among commodities produced this effect.[11]

11. G. Fiaccavento, "L'imposta sul valore aggiunto come strumento di perequazione tributaria" (The Value-Added Tax as an Instrument of Tax Equalization), *Rivista di Politica Economica*, vol. 63 (October 1973), pp. 34–48. This incidence analysis was based on data from the family expenditure survey of 1971 by the Central Statistical Office.

Table 4. Value-Added Taxes as a Percentage of Consumption Expenditure and of Income, 1978

Average income (thousands of lire)	*Tax as percent of consumption*[a]			*Taxes as percent of income*[b]		
	Total	*Necessities*	*Luxuries*	*Total*	*Necessities*	*Luxuries*
1,339	5.2	4.1	11.2	4.9	3.2	1.7
2,908	6.3	4.5	11.0	5.6	2.9	2.7
5,240	7.0	4.7	10.8	6.0	2.5	3.5
7,328	7.4	4.9	10.6	6.1	2.2	3.9
8,448	7.5	4.9	10.5	6.1	2.1	4.0
10,734	7.8	5.0	10.4	6.3	1.9	4.4
19,983	9.4	5.0	11.5	7.4	1.3	6.1

Source: G. Salvemini, *Imposta sul valore aggiunto e distribuzione del reddito* (Value-Added Tax and Income Distribution) (Rome: Bank of Italy, Research Department, 1980), tables 2.2.1 and 2.2.3.

a. Tax is measured as a percentage of consumption expenditure in each category. Tax as a percentage of total expenditure is a weighted average of the percentages for necessities and luxuries.

b. Tax in each category is measured as a percentage of total income. Tax on total expenditures is the simple sum of the rates on necessities and luxuries.

Table 4 presents estimates of value-added tax burdens based on the rates prevailing in 1978.[12] Whether value-added tax burdens are related to income or to consumption expenditure, the tax is somewhat progressive. These effects arise because commodities taxed at higher rates constitute an increasing fraction of household expenditures as one moves up the income scale and because consumption is a smaller fraction of high than of low incomes.

Conclusion

Italian experience with the value-added tax dramatizes the incompatibility between tax equity—both horizontal and vertical—and efficient administration. In designing its value-added tax, Italy sought to avoid major changes in tax liabilities from those under the preexisting turnover tax. It also sought to make the value-added tax progressive relative to both consumption expenditure and income. It succeeded in achieving both objectives by adopting a tax with highly varied rates and with exemptions. But in achieving these objectives, it sacrificed simplicity. Under the best of circumstances, the lack of systematic record-keeping in many

12. G. Salvemini, *Imposta sul valore aggiunto e distribuzione del reddito* (Value-Added Tax and Income Distribution) (Bank of Italy, Research Department, 1980). This study is based on a comparison of data from the family budget survey of 1978 by the Central Statistical Office with data from the Bank of Italy's survey of income distribution for the same year.

parts of the Italian economy would have made administration difficult and evasion easy. The complexity of the Italian value-added tax put an additional obstacle in the path of efficient administration and, although precise estimates are lacking, undoubtedly increased evasion. Whether a similar trade-off would plague countries with greater documentation of economic transactions must be left to the judgment of experts knowledgeable about those countries.

SIJBREN CNOSSEN

The Netherlands

THE NETHERLANDS introduced a consumption-type value-added tax on January 1, 1969, in compliance with directives of the Council of Ministers of the European Economic Community. This paper reviews the history of sales taxation in the Netherlands, describes the particular value-added tax adopted and the way it is administered, and presents evidence on the social and economic effects of the tax.

Sales Taxation

Sales taxation in the Netherlands dates back to the Spanish *alcavala,* a turnover tax introduced in the Low Countries in 1571 by the Duke of Alva to help finance the army that was to put down the Dutch rebellion.[1] Recent history with sales taxation began in 1934 with the adoption of a single-stage manufacturers' sales tax to finance budget deficits incurred during the depression of the 1930s. In 1941, shortly after the German occupation of the Netherlands began, a multistage turnover tax that strongly resembled the 1934 turnover tax in Germany was introduced. The cascade features of the tax were retained following the enactment of a similar Dutch tax in 1954. It was thought that this change would facilitate the envisaged elimination of border adjustments applied to imports from Belgium and Luxembourg, the other members of the Benelux customs union. For administrative reasons, retailers were exempted from the tax. The general rate was set at 5 percent, somewhat higher than the rate

1. Commonly referred to as the "tenth penny," the monstrous levy aroused support for a continuation of the revolt. For more on this tax, see Geoffrey Parker, *The Dutch Revolt* (Penguin, 1979), pp. 114–15.

under the previous sales tax, which had included the retail stage, but certain basic commodities—foods, shoes, household fuel, and some other goods—were exempted. Luxury rates of 7 and 15 percent were applied to specified commodities. Some effort was made to reduce the advantage of integrated firms by requiring them to pay tax on goods produced and used within a given firm.

Over time the turnover tax became so unwieldy (particularly after attempts at simplification) that allegedly only its principal draftsman was fully cognizant of all the intricacies.[2] Complexities flowed from attempts to mitigate the cascade effects of the tax, as well as to settle the numerous definitional issues raised by exemptions and by the differential taxation of various commodities. The fact that different rates were imposed on wholesalers and manufacturers led to extensive litigation over the class to which particular firms belonged. Discontent increased as rates rose, as well as because the tax at the import stage and the refund at the export stage did not take account of the tax on capital goods, a shortcoming that pinched increasingly as remaining border taxes were gradually eliminated by the European Economic Community and exports—for instance, of steel, chemical products, oil, and paper—became more capital-intensive.

Even before the EEC's directives on the value-added tax, the Dutch Ministry of Finance circulated a draft proposal to representatives of the business community and trade unions, inviting their comments. A bill was sent to the parliament in the fall of 1967. Debates centered mainly on exemptions, rate reductions, and the advisability of increased rates to alter the distribution of tax burdens. Goods favored under the turnover tax received similar treatment under the value-added tax. Political objections to taxing the retail stage were eventually overcome. Adoption of a value-added tax of the net income type was considered but rejected. After passage into law in June 1968, an extensive campaign of public education on the value-added tax began. The ministry organized seminars, issued manuals and pamphlets, and rounded off the campaign with thirteen ten-minute television programs.

2. H. Schuttevâer, quoted in J. Reugebrink, *Omzetbelasting* (Sales Tax), 2d ed. (Deventer, Netherlands: FED, 1979), p. 36. Some believed that there was more than one expert who understood the tax, but everyone agreed that they could be counted on the fingers of one hand. Two of them—A. E. de Moor and J. B. van der Zanden, who became acknowledged experts on the value-added tax also—reviewed an earlier draft of this paper.

Transitional measures were necessary to eliminate certain problems of double taxation that otherwise would have arisen when the value-added tax was introduced. The turnover tax on goods held as stock in trade was refunded for a two-year period following the adoption of the value-added tax. The tax on immovable property was refundable at 8 percent. All in all, 223,000 refunds were made, involving 1.6 billion guilders, or 32 percent of turnover tax receipts in 1968.[3] An immediate full credit for the value-added tax on capital goods would have involved a revenue loss of 5 billion guilders, a sacrifice the government was not prepared to make. Accordingly, a temporary investment levy was imposed. Such a tax was necessary also to reduce the incentive for businessmen to defer investment, which was subject to the turnover tax but not to the value-added tax.[4] The levy, which was phased out after four years, yielded 3.8 billion guilders, or 13 percent of value-added tax receipts from 1969 to 1972.

Value-Added Tax Base and Structure

Although the Dutch value-added tax complies with the directives of the European Economic Community, it has certain features that distinguish it from those of other EEC members. These features must be understood before one can address the economic and social effects of the tax and the administrative problems it poses.

The Tax Base

The Netherlands exports and imports roughly half of its gross domestic product (see table 1). As a result, nearly one-fourth of gross value-added tax receipts is refunded, and the fraction would be even higher if taxes on most imports and export-related services were not suspended. Furthermore, roughly one-third of consumption is exempted or cannot properly be considered part of the tax base. Another feature of the consumption-type value-added tax is that nearly one-fourth of the actual tax base consists of investment expenditure, a fact that cannot readily be inferred from the law. A large part of the tax is collected on intermediate and capital

3. See J. B. van der Zanden, *Wet op de Omzetbelasting, 1968* (Law on the Sales Tax, 1968) (Deventer: Kluwer, loose-leaf), articles 43, 45.

4. Certain investment goods were exempt from the levy because they had not previously been subject to turnover tax or were used in depressed sectors. The exempt goods included ships, airplanes, and textile and shoe machinery.

Table 1. Value-Added Tax Base in 1977

Item	Billions of guilders
Gross domestic product	**261.4**
Add: Imports	127.4
Deduct: Exports	130.7
Total expenditures	**258.1**
Private consumption expenditure	153.8
Government consumption expenditure	47.6
Fixed capital formation	54.8
Increase in business inventories	1.8
Excludable expenditures	**116.7**
Government wages and salaries	21.0[a]
Government sales, depreciation (net)	−0.2
Fixed capital formation	23.4[b]
Increase in business inventories	1.8
Consumption abroad (net)	2.9
Exemptions	48.1
Newspapers (zero rated)	0.8
Value-added tax	18.9[c]
Value-added tax base[d]	**141.4**
Consumption	109.0
Investment	32.4
Subject to 4 percent tax	46.8
Subject to 18 percent tax	94.6

Sources: Centraal Bureau voor de Statistiek (Central Bureau of Statistics), *Nationale Rekeningen, 1979* (National Accounts, 1979) (The Hague: Staatsuitgeverij, 1980), tables 21, 22, 37, 39, 40; and table 2, below. Figures are rounded.

a. Except wages and salaries of educational institutions, which have been taken as a proxy for educational services rendered.

b. Gross fixed capital formation minus taxable capital investment expenditure shown in table 2 (including tax).

c. Actual receipts were 19.3 billion guilders. The difference can be explained by the use of data on commodity flows rather than household budgets, the application of the rates to broad categories of goods and services, and lags in collections.

d. Total expenditures less excludable expenditures.

goods bought by exempted firms, on fixed assets of government, and on new residential buildings. As a result, the value-added tax is not free of the cascade effects and attendant distortions of consumption and investment that are widely thought to have disappeared with the termination of the turnover tax. One-half of the tax base is subject to the "normal" rate of 18 percent, the other half of value added is exempt, zero rated, or taxed at 4 percent (see table 2).

Table 3 shows various effective average rates of tax on private and public consumption and investment.

Rates

The most notable change in the value-added tax since its inception has been the large, rapid increase in the general tax rate: from 12 percent in 1969 to 14 percent in 1971, 16 percent in 1973, and finally 18 percent in 1976. Revenues rose from 4.5 billion guilders (4.8 percent of gross domestic product) in 1969 to 22.4 billion guilders (8.3 percent of gross domestic product) in 1979. The value-added tax now represents one-sixth of total revenue. The rate of tax expressed as a percentage of the actual tax base is 13.6 (table 1).

It is noteworthy that the 4 percent reduced rate has not been increased concurrently with the normal rate. The reduced rate applies to fifty categories of goods and fifteen categories of services.[5] Initially, the list consisted mainly of goods important in the budgets of low-income households, but administrative considerations and the achievement of other objectives required the addition of various income-elastic items.[6] From time to time, the question arises whether new products are eligible for the reduced rate. Often decisions have to be taken that are at variance with the objective of the reduced rate.[7]

Exemptions

The exemptions under the Dutch value-added tax conform broadly to those permitted under the sixth directive of the EEC. Health services, rents and imputed rents, education and welfare activities, insurance, banking, postal services, and broadcasting are all exempt from tax, al-

5. More than half the value of all lower rated commodities consists of foods, practically all of which are taxed at 4 percent, except items such as sweets, ice cream, and sugar, which are taxed at the normal rate. See also table 2.

6. Initially, food, coffee, and tea served in hotels and restaurants were taxed at the normal rate, but to improve the tourist balance they were made subject to the reduced rate. However, to reduce the revenue loss, deductions of prior-stage tax on these items were terminated.

7. For instance, expensive meat is taxed at 4 percent but expensive fish at 18 percent. Prepared meals are taxed at the lower rate, but pancakes, fish and chips, and salads bear the normal rate unless they are consumed in hotels or restaurants, where they are taxed like all other foods at 4 percent. Obviously, these examples do not make for an internally consistent value-added tax.

though producers of these exempt services are allowed no credit for prior-stage taxes.

The Netherlands, like other EEC countries, has opted for separate selective taxes on insurance, share issues, and brokerage. This alternative form of taxation of exempt activities reduces administrative burdens under the value-added tax. But the goal is not achieved because most banks, insurance companies, and other financial institutions also perform taxable activities. As a result, the computation of the tax base involves difficult problems in the allocation of expenses.

Table 2. The Value-Added Tax Structure in 1977

Billions of guilders before tax unless otherwise specified

	Expenditures			
Rate category	*Private*	*Government*	*Total*	*Percent of total*
Zero rate	**0.8**[a]	**0.0**	**0.8**	**0.4**
Exemptions	**33.3**	**14.8**	**48.1**	**25.3**
Health services	16.0	0.0	16.0	
Rents	14.1	0.0	14.1	
Education	0.0	14.1[b]	14.1	
Social services	3.9	0.0	3.9	
Insurance, banks	3.7[c]	0.0	3.7	
Postal services	1.9	0.5	2.4	
Other services	0.3	0.2	0.5	
Small businesses	0.4[d]	0.0	0.4	
Taxable intermediate goods	−7.0[e]	0.0	−7.0	
Tax of 4 percent	**43.7**	**3.1**	**46.8**	**24.6**
Consumption	42.4	3.1	45.5	
Food products	22.4	0.0	22.4	
Fuels[f]	4.2	1.0	5.2	
Hotels, restaurants	4.1	0.0	4.1	
Water, coffee, tea	2.8	0.0	2.8	
Public transportation	2.0	0.7	2.7	
Books, periodicals	2.1	0.0	2.1	
Entertainment, recreation	2.1	0.0	2.1	
Medicaments	1.4	0.0	1.4	
Flowers, plants	1.3	0.0	1.3	
Other services	0.0	1.4[g]	1.4	
Investment	1.3	0.0	1.3	
Agriculture, fixed assets	0.8[h]	0.0	0.8	
Intermediate goods of exempt sectors	0.5[h]	0.0	0.5	

Table 2 (*continued*)

Rate category	*Expenditures*			*Percent of total*
	Private	*Government*	*Total*	
Tax of 18 percent	**80.0**	**14.6**	**94.6**	**49.7**
Consumption	56.1	7.4	63.5	
Investment	23.9	7.2	31.1	
Housing	12.8	0.0	12.8	
Government, fixed assets	0.0	7.2[h,i]	7.2	
Agriculture, fixed assets	1.7[h]	0.0	1.7	
Exempt sectors, fixed assets	3.9[h]	0.0	3.9	
Intermediate goods of exempt sectors	5.5[h]	0.0	5.5	
Total	**157.8**	**32.5**	**190.3**	**100.0**

Source: Same as table 1.

a. Newspapers sold by subscription. The zero rate was terminated at the end of 1979. At present newspapers are subject to the 4 percent rate.

b. Wages and salaries of educational institutions, which have been taken as a proxy for educational services rendered.

c. Excluding interest margins of banks totaling 8.2 billion guilders.

d. The sum of (1) the number of exempt small businesses × (gross profit less taxable purchases) is 10.055 × (F 41.464 − 50 percent of F 21.464) = F 0.31 billion, plus (2) the number of small businesses × the average exemption is 74.536 × F 1.057 = F 0.08 billion; total exemption, F 0.39 billion.

e. Including 1.0 billion guilders in value-added tax.

f. Subject to 18 percent tax as of April 1, 1978.

g. Transfers of the government to nonprofit institutions.

h. Data supplied by the Central Bureau of Statistics.

i. Excluding investments by the government of 0.5 billion guilders.

Instead of taxing rents and rental values, as theoretically should be done, the Netherlands has elected to apply the tax only to the transfer of newly improved property within two years after initial use. The tax is considered final if the property is sold to a private person. If the property is transferred after two years, but within nine years, part of the credit for prior-stage taxes is repayable. The tax applies also to investments by the government in roads, bridges, and land that is being cleared or developed. Clearly, the application of the value-added tax to such assets is little more than an exercise in bookkeeping. All immovable property not covered by the value-added tax is subject to a 6 percent transfer tax.[8]

Special exemptions apply to the agricultural sector and small businesses. Farmers do not pay tax on the sale of their produce, but neither can they take credit for prior-stage tax on inputs. As a result, the agri-

8. Since the liability for both the transfer tax and the value-added tax occurs at transfer, some problems have arisen in determining which tax should be applicable. See Reugebrink, *Omzetbelasting*, pp. 253–57.

Table 3. Effective Rates of the Value-Added Tax on Private and Public Consumption and Investment, 1977

Amounts in billions of guilders

Type of expenditure	*Amount of base*	*Amount of tax*	*Tax as percent of base*
Consumption	152.2	14.3	9.4
Private	141.0	12.8[a]	9.1
Government	11.2[b]	1.5	13.4
Fixed capital	50.2	4.6	9.2
Residential	12.8	2.3	18.0
Other private	29.7	1.0	3.4
Government	7.7[c]	1.3	16.9
Total or average	202.4	18.9	9.3

Source: Same as table 1.
a. Including value-added tax on intermediate goods of exempt sectors.
b. Material consumption expenditures.
c. Including investment expenditures by the government.

cultural sector largely remains outside the value-added tax system. However, to avoid cumulative effects (after all, the chain has been broken and prior-stage taxes would be added to subsequent prices), purchasers of agricultural products are allowed an imputed credit of 4.5 percent of their purchases against the tax payable on sales. Purportedly this credit represents the average tax borne on agricultural inputs. As long as the prior-stage tax approximately equals the rate of tax on direct sales to consumers, no distortion should arise. Farmers may choose taxation if their prior-stage tax exceeds 4.5 percent of their sales. In 1979 some 10 percent of all farmers exercised this option.

Small businesses are partially or wholly exempt depending on the net tax they would have to pay if not exempt. This criterion appears more satisfactory than one based on turnover, although it favors small businesses selling goods subject to the reduced rate.

Exports and Imports

According to the destination principle embodied in the Dutch and all other European value-added taxes, exports are zero rated and imports are subject to tax on the same basis as if they were produced domestically. However, the unusual importance of international trade in the Dutch economy has led to a number of special features. "Rotterdam freer than a free port" is the time-honored maxim underlying the treatment of exports and imports under the value-added tax. Transit goods are not considered imported and hence are not subject to value-added tax. Services connected with international trade, such as transportation, loading and unloading, and warehousing, are zero rated, as are services performed for carriers, such as repairing, leasing, towing, piloting, and salvaging, and this provision is interpreted liberally. Upgrading of goods for export, through blending, repacking, or labeling, is also zero rated. To reduce red tape and carrying costs, value-added tax on more than 95 percent of all imports is collected inland rather than at the border.

Administration and Compliance

Dutch experience with the value-added tax suggests that the so-called built-in self-enforcement aspect of the tax, which permits the matching of the tax credits of one taxpayer against the tax payable of another, is a much overrated advantage. The compliance record indicates that administrative staff has devoted a large part of its time to ensuring that returns are filed on time and to rechecking claims for refunds.

Returns and Assessments

In 1979 some 434,000 firms filed nearly 2.2 million returns. Sixty-two percent of all firms file quarterly returns, but large firms must file monthly and small firms may file annually. Nearly one-fifth of all returns call for refunds; these totaled 7.5 billion guilders in 1979, or nearly one-third of net tax receipts. Most refunds are related to exports, but some are caused by the wide margin between the normal rate some firms pay on inputs and the reduced rate on their outputs. Most firms are required to keep records on an accrual basis, but some shopkeepers, retail outlets, and specially designated businesses are permitted to use cash accounting.

If a return is not filed on time, the taxpayer makes an error, or an examination of his records reveals that he has underpaid, an assessment is levied by the taxing authorities. Some 253,000 assessments, or one for every eight returns, involving 10 percent of net tax receipts, were issued in 1979. Most of these assessments are pro forma notices based on presumed late payment. Not surprisingly, six out of ten lead to a time-consuming objection; approximately half of the tax assessed is then reduced.

Although there are no studies on compliance costs, no doubt taxpayer obligations under the value-added tax are most onerous for small businesses in the Netherlands. Because of diversity in sales, difficulties in accounting for different rates of tax are most serious at the retail stage. At this stage also there are the problems of keeping track of deposits on bottles, as well as of stamps and value coupons. These considerations imply that compliance costs are almost certainly distributed regressively with respect to income. To be sure, small businesses are entitled to an exemption in the form of a deduction from tax of at most 2,050 guilders, but this compensation appears inadequate in view of the extra administrative costs.

Evasion

A recent government report on tax fraud casts considerable light on the problem of tax evasion.[9] This report is based on 77,000 field audits conducted in 1976. As a result of these audits, 45,000 additional assessments were issued, yielding 310 million guilders in additional revenue, almost 2 percent of receipts for that year. The report revealed that fraud was slightly more frequent at the retail stage than at other stages of production, but that less revenue was involved than at other stages.

More important, 34 percent of all the firms that had their accounts audited had evaded tax, and these evasions amounted to 1.2 percent of receipts. Forty-four percent of all adjustments for tax evasion involved deliberately incorrect applications of the law, such as rules regarding deductions for prior-stage taxes. Sixteen percent had tried to postpone payment improperly. Thirty-eight percent had failed to enter sales in their books or had kept incomplete accounts. Seven out of ten violations were committed by former offenders, perhaps because the penalties for violation tend to be rather low.[10]

The report estimated that if all returns had been audited, approximately 870 million guilders in additional revenue would have been collected. The period covered in the audits was more than one year, however. On the other hand, the report was based on examinations of existing files and thus excluded a fairly large amount of tax evaded at the retail stage, primarily through nonreporting of such taxable services as painting, plumbing, and

9. W. J. van Bijsterveld, "Aangepaste versie van het verslag van een onderzoek naar de aard en de omvang van de belastingfraude" (Adjusted Version of the Report of a Survey on the Nature and Extent of Tax Evasion) (The Hague: Staatsuitgeverij, April 1980), chap. 7 and pp. 254–57.

10. Of all assessments imposed in 1976, half led to no penalty, only 2 percent led to penalties of 25 percent of tax due, and fewer than 0.2 percent led to penalties equal to tax due, the largest penalty imposed. Ibid., p. 195.

carpentry. The report concluded that greater penalties should be imposed, particularly on repeating offenders.

Compliance may improve beginning in 1981, when data from imports will be computerized, a step that will make it easier to match invoices. Too much should not be expected, however, as such a step will cover only transactions that are reported to the authorities, not those that are performed outside the tax framework. That this problem may be serious is suggested by experience in Belgium, where 8 percent of value-added tax is evaded even though all data on imports are put into computers and matched.[11]

Economic and Social Aspects

The analysis of the tax base and structure shows that the value-added tax in practice is not a simple, uniform tax on all consumption. It is important to keep this in mind in considering the effects of the tax on income distribution, resource allocation, and prices. The value-added tax falls in part on investment, and with different weight on various consumption goods and hence on different consumers. The differences in rates among consumer goods create excise-type tax effects that alter relative prices. Such changes in relative prices can cause demand for various goods to change and lead to the movement of factors of production among industries, with attendant changes in factor prices. Although such effects may be important, there is no evidence and all empirical work ignores them. Nevertheless, the maxim that consumers bear the burden of the value-added tax may not be entirely accurate, and the distribution of the portion of the burden they bear may be much more complex than is ordinarily assumed.

Distribution

The Dutch legislature tried to design the value-added tax so that its burden would be distributed in the same way as that of the turnover tax. This goal led to reduced rates for food products and agricultural inputs and exemptions for important services. The Central Planning Bureau estimated that the value-added tax would be slightly less regressive with

11. See "Prof. M. Frank over belastingontduiking en fiscale onderschatting" (Prof. M. Frank on Tax Evasion and Tax Underestimation), *Maandblad Belastingbeschouwingen,* vol. 49 (July–August 1980), pp. 154–55.

respect to income than the turnover tax had been.[12] The bureau concluded on the basis of 1963–65 household budget surveys that the increase in the cost of living from the value-added tax would be 1.2 percent for those with annual incomes of 6,000–9,000 guilders and 1.6 percent for those with incomes in excess of 20,000 guilders. Broader coverage of services under the value-added tax than under the turnover tax produced this progressive differential effect. The bureau also found that the increase in the tax burden on large families was somewhat smaller than that on small families. This study indicates that the conversion of the turnover tax to the value-added tax was mildly progressive.

A further study based on 1974–75 household budget surveys of working families showed that the value-added tax as a percentage of income declined from 8 percent of incomes below 21,000 guilders to 7.5 percent of incomes over 21,000 guilders.[13] With the same data base, a recent study confirmed these findings. Specifically, it was found that the value-added tax burden decreased from 9.3 percent for family incomes below 16,000 guilders to 6.7 percent for incomes above 44,000 guilders.[14] These studies therefore indicate that the replacement of the value-added tax with a proportional income tax would be progressive. The estimates disregard expenditures on new houses and foreign travel (taxed abroad), however; if these items had been included in the survey, the Dutch value-added tax would probably have been distributed roughly in proportion to income over most of the income range.

The Dutch attempt to mitigate the income regressivity of the value-added tax by exemptions and reduced rates largely succeeded, but it is hard to justify such an effort in a country well equipped with alternative instruments for reducing income inequality. The Netherlands has gone a

12. Parliamentary proceedings, *Tweede Kamer der Staten-General* (Second Chamber of the States-General), session 1967–68: 9324, 9410, Memorie van Antwoord (Note of Reply), app. 6, pp. 12–14.

13. B. de Vet, "De druk van BTW en accijnzen voor werknemersgezinnen in de periode mei 1974–april 1975" (The Burden of the Value-Added Tax and Excises for Employees' Families in the Period May 1974–April 1975), *Sociale Maandstatistiek,* no. 8 (1978), pp. 730–37. Actually, de Vet computed the burden with respect to total consumption expenditures, but the figures can be readily related to incomes, which are also given.

14. R. Goudriaan, F. G. van Herwaarden and C. A. de Kam, "De drukverdeling van omzetbelasting en accijnzen, 1974–1975" (The Distribution of the Burden of the Sales Tax and Excises, 1974–1975), *Economisch Statistische Berichten* (February 11, 1981), pp. 128–33.

long way toward reducing income inequality by other means.[15] Rather a strong case can be made for having a truly broad-based value-added tax, encompassing as many goods and services as possible and taxing them all at the same rate.[16] Possible regressive effects can be offset through transfer payments or adjustments in other taxes. The use of multiple rates and exemptions increases administrative burdens to crudely achieve a set of distributional goals that can be achieved more precisely by available alternative devices.

Neutrality

Although the value-added tax is superior to the turnover tax, it is not as universal and neutral as is often believed. Exemptions and reduced rates make serious inroads into the potential tax base. The value-added tax covers services (professional and transportation services, for example) more completely than the turnover tax did, but the important categories of health, education, and finance remain exempt. The element of non-deductible tax surely is an imperfect substitute for the tax that would have been payable but for the exemption. This tax will be reflected unsystematically in prices, and it may be assumed that labor-intensive services will be favored over capital-intensive services.

In practice, exemptions may favor large firms over small ones, because large firms to some extent can integrate the provision of medical, dental, or insurance services with their main line of business and thereby receive credit for prior-stage taxes. Similarly, banks would save interest on the tax by channeling their capital-intensive services, such as the use of computer facilities, through taxable subsidiaries. And tax would be avoided if the subsidiaries' services are not valued "at arm's length" (determined by market forces). Furthermore, exempt institutions such as hospitals are induced to perform laundry, cleaning, and administrative services themselves rather than buy them from outside contractors in order to avoid payment of prior-stage taxes. The law empowers the Minister of Finance

15. Income inequality was reduced more than 50 percent between 1938 and 1976. J. Pen and J. Tinbergen, *Naar een rechtvaardiger inkomensverdeling* (Toward a More Equitable Distribution of Income) (Amsterdam: Elsevier, 1977), chap. 1, especially pp. 49–51.

16. Clearly, selective excises on such commodities as alcohol and tobacco and user charges such as effluent fees and congestion taxes deliberately imposed to alter consumption or to internalize external effects still have their place and can be justified.

to tax such services, but thus far the provision has not been invoked; administrative problems loom large here.

It is difficult to tax current housing services, but new residential construction is covered. A tax on new housing investment, however, is a poor substitute for a tax on services provided by the existing housing stock. But the housing market is subject to such pervasive controls that the full effects of any tax would be hard to estimate. The rents of most houses are fully controlled, and land and structures are often subsidized. Neither the actual tax nor one more accurately based on value added would necessarily be reflected in prices.

The tax on government investments does not show up directly in prices at all. Subsidies for fixed assets in the private sector are yet another element that may infringe neutrality; if not included in taxable value, they may distort prices of subsidized goods and of other goods for which they are inputs, but if they are included in taxable value, they would be difficult to distinguish from loans on easy terms or hidden subsidies in government contracts.

The lack of information about price elasticities of supply and demand for products and factors makes any complete assessment of the effects of reduced rates difficult. Although the demand for essential foods is fairly inelastic and hence the distortion is relatively small, the demand for fruit, fish, expensive meat, flowers, admissions, and hotel and restaurant services is known to respond to price changes. The lower tax on these commodities therefore should influence demand and supply, as well as wages and payments to owners of capital in higher taxed industries. The distortions caused by the lower rate are probably the most serious, because one-fourth of the tax base is subject to that rate and because prices of exempt services are largely determined outside the market anyway.

Price Effects

At the time the value-added tax was introduced the Central Planning Bureau estimated that the tax would boost prices by 1.4 percent in the first year, but that the effect after three years would be less than 1 percent.

Although the average effect on prices of replacing the turnover tax with the value-added tax was expected to be small, the effective tax rates on different goods and services were expected to change significantly. If reflected in product prices, therefore, the change in taxes would alter relative prices paid by consumers and producers. The computations of the bureau convincingly proved the existence of large unintended distortions

Table 4. Contribution of the Value-Added Tax and of Other Factors to Inflation, 1969–80

Consumption year	*Nature of change in value-added tax*	*Contribution to change in price index of family consumption*[a] *From value-added tax*	*From other factors*	*Total*
1969	Introduction of value-added tax	1.4	6.1	7.5
1970	Postponement of refund of tax on inventories and phase-in of capital goods credit	...	4.4	4.4
1971	Two-point rate increase; transfer of some commodities to reduced rate	0.6	6.4	7.0
1972	Transfer of some commodities to reduced rate; electricity taxed at normal rate	0.1	7.9	8.0
1973	Two-point rate increase	1.2	6.8	8.0
1974	None	...	9.5	9.5
1975	Transfer of some goods to reduced rate	...	10.0	10.0
1976	Two-point rate increase; transfer of some commodities to reduced rate	0.7	8.3	9.0
1977	None	...	6.5	6.5
1978	Application of normal rate to fuels	0.3	3.7	4.0
1979	Adjustment to sixth directive	...	4.0–4.5	4.0–4.5
1980	Newspapers subject to reduced rate	...	6.5–7.0	6.5–7.0

Sources: Centraal Planbureau (Central Planning Bureau), *Macro-economische verkenning* (Macro-economic Review) (The Hague: Staatsuitgeverij), selected years; and Ministerie van Financiën (Ministry of Finance), *Memorie van Toelichting* (Explanatory Note), selected years.

a. Change from preceding year.

under the old turnover tax. To the extent that the value-added tax raised a greater proportion of a given revenue from consumption than the turnover tax had, the quantity of consumer goods demanded domestically would decline, thereby freeing capacity for export markets, but the actual magnitude of such effects has not been estimated.

The total effect of the introduction of and changes in the value-added tax on the price index of family consumption has been estimated by the Central Planning Bureau and is shown in table 4. In 1969 the total price increase was 1.5 percentage points higher than originally estimated, largely because the introduction of the tax coincided with a cyclical rise of economic activity. Firms may also have seized the opportunity to widen gross profit margins. The bureau stuck to its estimate of the part of the overall price increase that it attributed to the changeover. The table makes clear that the introduction of the value-added tax and subsequent increases in rates have added only marginally to inflationary pressures and have not been a major factor in Dutch inflation.[17]

Conclusion

Based on Dutch experience, efforts to incorporate equity considerations into the design of a value-added tax seem misplaced. The value-added tax is an effective device for raising large amounts of revenue without distorting consumption decisions, but equity goals can be achieved more naturally and without creating serious administrative problems with the income tax and through transfers. In designing the value-added tax, microeconomic effects should be heeded; distortions in production and consumption should be avoided.

On most counts, the value-added tax in the Netherlands should be considered an improvement over the turnover tax it replaced. The base of the value-added tax is broader, it permits more precise border adjustments (a major advantage in a small open economy), it is reasonably well accepted, and enforcement problems are manageable. The changeover was exceptionally well executed and "teething problems" were solved expeditiously.

The neutrality of the tax would be improved, however, if the coverage of services was broadened and if exemptions were replaced by zero rating, although such a step is contrary to the directives of the European Economic Community. Increased use of zero rating rather than exemptions would reduce the advantage that large firms have over small firms.

The use of reduced rates should also be curtailed. The Netherlands has an ample number of instruments for altering the income distribution that

17. Based on data in table 4, if the Dutch consumer price index stood at 100 at the beginning of 1969, it had risen to 203.7 at the end of 1978; without the value-added tax it would have stood at 195.7, 8 percentage points or 7.7 percent lower than the increase that occurred.

would not distort consumer choices. The use of reduced rates is partly self-defeating anyway, as administrative considerations frequently cause the favorable rates to be assigned to goods disproportionately consumed by upper income groups. Unification of the two rates at 13 to 14 percent would raise the family consumption price index by about 0.6 percentage point.

A number of other changes in the value-added tax should be made. Agriculture should be taxed like other industries, but if special rates are to be retained, it would be better if sales by farmers were zero rated and if the special arrangements applicable to them were abolished; such a step would cause value-added tax refunds to match the actual taxes that farmers incur. There is little rationale for taxing government expenditures on fixed assets; properly designed and administered benefit taxes would seem more appropriate in most cases.

Even if these changes were made, a well-designed retail sales tax would have the important advantage over the value-added tax of promoting tax consciousness. If the medium is the message, placing the full tax on consumer purchases might heighten awareness of what government costs. It has perhaps been too easy to increase the value-added tax whenever the need for additional revenue arose. Within the Common Market, a retail sales tax would permit greater intercountry variations in tax design and obviate the need for border adjustments. The principal disadvantages of the retail sales tax are that evasion is likely to be somewhat greater than under a value-added tax and that the treatment of certain investment goods may be more uneven.[18]

One motive for the introduction of a value-added tax in the United States is a desire to use some or all of the proceeds to reduce other taxes. If Dutch experience is any guide, such shifts, however desirable they may be in theory, would not occur. Rather the tax ratio would probably increase in line with the new tax.

18. Following the harmonization of the value-added tax bases and rates, supplementary retail sales taxes might be used by member states wishing to exploit this source of revenue more fully.

GÖRAN NORMANN

Sweden

IF MAJOR CHANGES in the tax structure of a country are unusual, then the past decade in Swedish fiscal history has been extraordinary. Taxes rose from 40.1 percent to 52.7 percent of gross national product, continuing a dramatic expansion in the role and cost of government services that has been going on since 1950. The composition of taxes changed in major ways with the introduction of the value-added tax, large increases in social security taxes, and basic changes in the structure of the personal income tax.

Because so much has been happening to Sweden's fiscal structure, it is difficult to sort out empirically the effect that the value-added tax has had on income distribution, prices, and other measures of economic performance. Nevertheless, some estimates have been made and are reported later in this paper. To facilitate understanding of the atmosphere within which decisions about the value-added tax were made, this paper first reviews the debates about taxation that led to the important changes in fiscal structure sketched above. Next it describes the value-added tax in Sweden, and presents such evidence as exists on the economic effects of the value-added tax. Finally, it briefly outlines reforms in the structure of value-added taxation now under consideration.

Fiscal Change

Between 1950 and 1970 the proportion of Swedish GNP captured by taxes doubled (see table 1). Roughly half of the increase was accounted for by growth in income taxes. The remainder was caused by growth of

Table 1. Selected Taxes as a Percentage of Gross National Product, 1950, 1960, 1970, and 1979

Tax	*Tax yield as percent of GNP (market prices)*			
	1950	*1960*	*1970*	*1979*
Personal income tax	9.9	12.7	18.6	22.7
Central government	4.8	6.4	8.2	7.4
Local government	5.1	6.3	10.4	15.3
Payroll taxes, including employers' contributions	0.4	3.7	8.6	15.8
Corporation income tax	3.0	2.4	1.8	1.5
Other direct taxes	0.9	0.8	0.7	0.6
Retail sales tax/value-added tax	...	1.5	4.2	7.0
Other indirect taxes	6.7	7.6	6.3	5.1
Total	20.9	28.7	40.2	52.7

Source: Statens Offentliga Utredningar (SOU), 1977:87 (Final Report by the Government Commission on Business Taxation). The 1979 figures are preliminary data from the Ministry of Budget Affairs.

payroll taxes and by the introduction of a retail sales tax in 1960 and its conversion to a value-added tax in 1969.

The Retail Sales Tax and the Value-Added Tax

Sweden experimented with a sales tax during the Second World War. Various committees consisting of members of parliament and of outside experts subsequently proposed different forms of indirect taxation. The parliament enacted a retail sales tax in 1959; it went into effect in 1960 at an initial rate of 4 percent. The base of the sales tax included not only consumption goods purchased by households, but also equipment purchased by businesses.

Only four years later a prestigious General Tax Commission proposed that the retail sales tax be replaced by a consumption-type value-added tax collected on the destination basis. The commission held that the value-added tax would be free of two flaws that marred the sales tax. Because the sales tax fell on business as well as household purchases, the commission argued, the incidence of the sales tax was unclear and the tax caused needless distortions in the allocation of resources. Because the ratio of investment to the value of final output varied among industries, the amount of tax borne by households would differ according to the types of goods they bought, and the changes in relative prices of these goods would cause wasteful reallocation of economic resources. While the validity of the commission's conclusions is open to serious question in light of subsequent analysis of tax incidence, this reasoning influenced its recommendations.

The commission leaned toward the value-added tax for a third reason, its belief that the revenue potential of the retail sales tax was far more limited than that of the value-added tax. The commission feared that the risk of tax evasion under a sales tax collected at a single stage was greater than it would be under a value-added tax collected successively in smaller individual amounts through the production cycle. Finally, the commission believed that the administrative difficulty of distinguishing taxable and nontaxable materials would be reduced under a value-added tax.

The value-added tax was introduced in 1969, initially at a rate of 10 percent. Rates rose in three steps, to 15 percent in 1971, 17.1 percent in 1977, and 19 percent in 1980.

Other Tax Developments

The increase in the value-added tax in 1971 was accompanied by major structural changes in the personal income tax. These changes included a shift from joint taxation of husbands and wives as a single taxable unit to individual taxation of spouses. This change is credited with encouraging a large increase in the labor force participation of married women.[1]

At the same time, the deductibility of local income taxes under the national income tax was repealed, and the overall progressivity of the income tax system was sharply increased. The former change meant that increases in local income taxes would no longer cause reductions in national tax collections. It also meant that increases in local income taxes would take an increased bite out of after-tax income, particularly for persons subject to relatively high marginal rates. Table 2 depicts the situation of an average industrial worker in 1968, before these changes were made, and in 1978, after they had been in effect for several years.

It is apparent that although an average worker's income tax rate (line 8) did not increase over the decade, his marginal rate (line 9) rose sig-

1. This is further discussed in Bertil Holmlund, "Perspektiv på arbetskraftsutbudets utveckling" (Perspectives on the Development of Labor Supply), in B. Axell and others, *Utrikeshandel, inflation och arbetsmarknad* (Foreign Trade, Inflation and the Labor Market) (Stockholm: Industrial Institute for Economic and Social Research, 1979).

Table 2. The Tax Situation for an Average Industrial Worker in 1968 and 1978[a]
Kronor unless otherwise specified

Item	*1968*	*1978*
1. Employers' cost	25,886	78,570
2. Payroll taxes	2,309	19,211
3. Income taxes	8,561	21,627
4. Average tax rate (percent) (rows 2 and 3 divided by row 1)	42.0	52.0
5. Marginal tax rate (percent) (corresponding to row 4)	55.9	72.0
6. Elasticity of income after tax (computed from rows 4 and 5)[b]	0.76	0.58
7. Paid-out wages (row 1 less row 2)	23,577	59,359
8. Average income tax rate (percent) (row 3 divided by row 7)	36.3	36.4
9. Marginal income tax rate (percent) (corresponding to row 8)	52.9	60.1
10. Elasticity of income after tax (computed from rows 8 and 9)[b]	0.74	0.63
11. Labor income after taxes (row 7 less row 3)	15,016	37,732
12. Indirect taxes[c]	1,802	8,287
13. Total taxes as a percent of employers' cost	50.0	62.5
14. Overall marginal tax rate (payroll, income, and indirect taxes as percent of employers' cost)	61.0	78.0

Source: Author's calculations with the Swedish TAX model. An early version of this model is described in Ulf Jakobsson and Göran Normann, "A Model of the Swedish System for Personal Income Taxation," *European Economic Review*, vol. 3, no. 4 (1972), pp. 451–67.

a. Adult, male, and working full time.

b. This elasticity shows the percentage change in income after tax when income before tax increases by 1 percent.

c. A rough estimate of general and specific consumption taxes.

nificantly; furthermore, the average total tax burden (line 13) increased even more, in part because of increases in payroll taxes and in part because of increases in indirect taxes (first the retail sales tax and then the value-added tax).

During the interval from 1972 to 1977 value-added tax rates were unchanged, but payroll tax rates were increased. In these years of especially active tax policy, the measures taken were frequently part of the wage bargaining process. The measures were preceded by negotiations between the ruling Social Democratic party, parts of the political opposition, and centralized unions. Concentration on payroll tax rates and wage rates permitted the negotiators to calculate with precision and negotiate over *after-tax* compensation. Partly because value-added taxes vary across families according to the proportion of income saved, they did not lend themselves to the bargaining process as it was carried out during this period. Annual agreements stipulated how much wages and payroll taxes would increase; these agreements included some reductions in personal income taxes imposed by the central government. It should be added that, because of wage drift, the actual wage change during the period usually deviated significantly from what was negotiated.

The Value-Added Tax

The Swedish value-added tax adheres broadly to the same principles as those of other European countries. Along with other Scandinavian countries, however, Sweden has avoided the highly differentiated rate structure that has complicated administration in other nations.

Structure

The value-added tax covers two-thirds of private consumption. The tax rate is nominally uniform, but partial or total exemptions and zero rating cause some differentiation in effective rates. For example, housing expenditures are exempt, but 60 percent of the value of newly built units is subject to tax. Only 20 percent of the value of roads, bridges, harbors, railways, playgrounds, and certain other commodities is subject to tax; the nearly complete exemption of this class of goods is intended to preserve the capacity of private contractors to compete with construction by public agencies and organizations.

The sellers of some commodities are exempt from taxation, but they are denied the right to claim refunds for taxes paid by their suppliers. The commodities in this category include residential rent, banking and insurance services, professional services, teaching, passenger transport, and entertainment, sports, and theatrical performances. Other exempt commodities include certain periodicals, works of art sold by the artist, and inventories transferred when a business is merged with another or sold.

A much larger class of goods is zero rated. This category includes boats and aircraft for professional use, munitions, prescription medicines, newspapers, electric power and other fuel (including that for automobiles), and all exports.

Services are taxable if the law explicitly lists them, but otherwise they are exempt (no refunds of taxes on suppliers are permitted). The main category of taxable services is that connected with taxable goods. Thus advertising, acquisition costs, storage, assembly, repair, maintenance, and alteration of commodities are all subject to tax. For similar reasons services connected with real property, such as work on grounds, forests, and buildings, are taxable.

Since September 8, 1980, the value-added tax rate has been 19 percent of the gross sales value of covered goods and services. Because the tax is included in the base, the rate defined net of tax is actually higher, 23.5 percent.[2]

Administration

Eligible taxpayers must submit tax returns every two months unless annual gross sales are less than 200,000 Swedish kronor (about $46,500 at late 1980 exchange rates), in which case they may file annually if they wish. Businesses with sales of less than 10,000 kronor (about $2,300) need not file returns at all, but this exemption is so low that even small farmers are included in the system. Sweden does not use the system employed by some members of the European Economic Community for excluding farmers from the value-added tax. The tax return is simple, requiring fourteen entries at most, and is filed through the post office.

The value-added tax yielded just under 30 billion kronor (after rebates) from 400,000 taxpayers in 1979 (see table 3); of this sum, somewhat less than 2 percent came from taxes imposed on purchases made by governments.[3] Most of the revenue is collected from a small minority of taxpayers; in fact, 3 percent of the taxpayers accounted for half of all revenue, and one-third of the taxpayers accounted for 95 percent of the revenue. Three agencies share responsibility for administering the value-added tax: the national tax board and two separate divisions of county administration.

For some time administration of the value-added tax has been subject to criticism. The parliament's standing committee on taxation declared in 1977 that much of the problem grew out of an underestimation of the

2. The tax as a percentage of the base excluding tax is $0.19/(1.0 - 0.19) = 0.2346$.

3. Author's estimate for 1975, using disaggregated national accounts data.

Table 3. Collection of the Value-Added Tax, 1969–79
Millions of kronor

Year	*Swedish customs*	*County administration*	*Total collected*	*VAT refunded*	*Net revenue*
1969	2,917	6,095	9,012	2,399	6,613
1970	3,545	6,260	9,805	2,872	6,933
1971	5,777	9,840	15,617	4,648	10,969
1972	6,375	11,276	17,651	5,136	12,315
1973	7,305	12,202	19,507	5,807	13,701
1974	9,198	12,959	22,157	7,828	14,329
1975	11,699	16,181	27,880	10,803	17,077
1976	13,162	18,624	31,786	11,013	20,773
1977	15,454	21,516	36,970	13,435	23,535
1978	16,748	25,488	42,236	15,084	27,152
1979	20,491	27,497	47,988	18,191	29,797

Source: National Tax Board, *Report 1*, MOMSORG Project (NTB, 1980).

problems of control when the transition from retail sales to value-added taxation occurred. Two committees are now working on proposals to improve administration, including extended use of automated data processing and better coordination among the agencies responsible for administering the tax.

Economic Effects: Prices

The Swedish National Bureau of Economic Research (Konjunkturinstitutet) has presented rough estimates of the contribution of various factors to inflation.[4] Table 4 shows the results of these estimates.

The estimates are rather mechanical, as they assume without proof the very issue to be resolved: that increases in value-added taxes are fully shifted forward in higher prices. Because roughly 60 percent of the consumption basket is subject to tax, a one percentage point increase in the value-added tax raises consumer prices about 0.6 percentage point. These estimates not only ignore the possibility that shifting may be incomplete, a possible upward bias in the estimates, but they also ignore

4. See *Konjunkturlaget* (The Swedish Economy), selected issues.

Table 4. Contribution of Indirect Taxes to Total Consumer Price Increase, 1969–80

Item	*1969*	*1970*	*1971*	*1972*	*1973*	*1974*	*1975*	*1976*	*1977*	*1978*	*1979*	*1980*
Total consumer price increase	4.8	7.0	7.5	5.7	7.6	10.5	10.1	9.4	12.8	7.5	9.7	14.0
Contribution of discretionary changes												
In the value-added tax } In other indirect taxes	0.1											
In the value-added tax		1.5	3.2	0.0	0.0	0.0	0.0	0.0	1.4	0.0	0.0	1.5
In other indirect taxes		0.0	0.0	−0.1	0.9	0.3	0.9	0.0	1.2	0.5	0.7	2.2
Contribution of automatic effect of the value-added tax	...	0.3	0.3	0.5	0.6	0.8	1.0	0.9	1.2	0.8	0.8	1.1
Share of the commodity basket covered by the value-added tax (percent)[a]	...	...	...	...	...	...	66.2	66.3	65.7	64.7	63.8	62.5

Source: Based on data supplied by Konjunkturinstitutet (Swedish National Institute of Economic Research).
a. These shares correspond to the weights used in calculations of the consumer price index and therefore refer to the situation in December, year $t - 1$.

possible indirect effects through market interactions and effects on wage settlements. A recent econometric study suggests that the value-added tax is fully translated into higher prices within one quarter; if correct, these findings indicate that the first source of bias is unimportant.[5]

The full effects on prices of increases in the value-added tax depend not only on the initial impact, but also on market interactions, the stage of the business cycle, and other policy measures. Simulations on a multi-equation econometric model suggest that an increase in the value-added tax in 1971 from 15 percent to 20 percent would have resulted in an increase in the implicit consumption deflator of roughly 2.5 percent after two years relative to what prices would have been if taxes had not been increased and all other policies were the same.[6] While these results are suggestive, the model on which they are based does not incorporate the institutional characteristics of the Swedish economy necessary for taking into account "cost-push" factors, such as labor supply adjustment and

5. Ingemar Hansson has estimated a price equation in which the quarterly percentage change in prices, $\dot{P}$, is a function of three seasonal dummy variables (S_2, S_3, and S_4), the rate of change of the value-added tax or of the retail sales tax ($CTAX$), capacity utilization ($MUTIL$), the rate of change of labor costs in nominal terms ($CNLC$), the average rate of change in real labor costs in the two preceding quarters ($CRLC_{12}$), average consumer price inflation in West Germany and the United States ($INTP$), and expected inflation determined by inflation rates in the ten preceding quarters (P_{-i}, $i = 1, \ldots, 10$). The estimated relation preferred by Hansson is as follows (standard errors are in parentheses):

$$\dot{P} = \underset{(0.444)}{-0.689} - \underset{(0.225)}{0.752}\, S_2 - \underset{(0.252)}{0.280}\, S_3 - \underset{(0.234)}{0.354}\, S_4 + \underset{(0.168)}{0.921}\, CTAX + \underset{(3.070)}{3.078}\, MUTIL$$

$$+ \underset{(3.128)}{1.978}\, MUTIL_{-1} + \underset{(0.039)}{0.091}\, CNLC + \underset{(0.103)}{0.072}\, CRLC_{12} + \underset{(0.239)}{0.578}\, INTP + \sum_{i=1}^{10} a_i P_{-i}.$$

$$\sum a_i = \underset{(0.202)}{0.713}; \text{ standard error} = 0.551; \bar{R}^2 = 0.736$$

See Ingemar Hansson, "Inflation in Sweden and the Effects of Price Controls," working paper (University of Lund, Department of Economics, 1980). The equation was estimated for the period from the first quarter of 1958 to the fourth quarter of 1976. An Almon lag structure was used. The coefficient of the value-added tax variable ranged from 1.020 to 0.90 in the five equations presented by Hansson.

6. This calculation is based on a model developed by the Econometric Research Unit at the Economic Research Institute of the Stockholm School of Economics. The model is described by Franz A. Ettlin, Johan A. Lybeck, Ingemar Erikson, Svante Johansson, and Björn Jarnhall, "The STEP 1 Quarterly Econometric Model of Sweden" (Stockholm: Economic Research Institute, Stockholm School of Economics, 1979). The estimate reported in the text is previously unpublished.

labor market negotiations in terms of real wages after taxes.[7] These factors are among the main issues in Swedish tax policy today.

Study of the impact of taxes on the rate of increase in wages is at an early stage. Sargan formulated the testable hypothesis that, if the rate of increase of real wages falls below a historically established norm, wage earners will try to increase money wages during the next negotiation to compensate for this.[8] Other British economists have explored this hypothesis further by formulating it in terms of after-tax real wages; they found that for the United Kingdom there is strong empirical evidence in support of the latter hypothesis.[9] The results of current research on related questions on Swedish data are so far somewhat inconclusive.[10] There are, however, some tentative results indicating that, as in the United

7. For a discussion of these factors, see D. A. L. Auld and Clive Southey, "The Simple Analytics of Tax Induced Inflation," *Public Finance,* vol. 32, no. 1 (1977), pp. 37–47; and Thorvaldur Gylfason and Assar Lindbeck, "Inflation and Macroeconomic Theory," seminar paper 133 (University of Stockholm, Institute for International Economic Studies, 1979).

8. See J. D. Sargan, "Wages and Prices in the United Kingdom: A Study in Econometric Methodology," in P. E. Hart, G. Mills, and J. K. Whitaker, eds., *Econometric Analysis for National Income Planning* (London: Butterworth, 1964), pp. 25–55.

9. S. G. B. Henry, M. C. Sawyer, and P. Smith, "Models of Inflation in the United Kingdom: An Evaluation," *National Institute Economic Review,* no. 77 (August 1976), pp. 60–71; and David Vines, "An Econometric Investigation of Annual Earnings Inflation in the United Kingdom, 1954–1975," Cambridge Growth Project Working Paper GDP 454 (Cambridge University, Department of Applied Economics, January 1978).

10. Among the equations fitted to annual Swedish data is the one given below (standard errors are in parentheses). The method of estimation is ordinary least squares; the time period is 1952–77:

$$\underset{}{\dot{W}} = 397.8 + \underset{(0.275)}{0.840\, t} + \underset{(2.63)}{2.98\, 1/u^2} + \underset{(0.138)}{0.514\, \dot{P}_{-1}} - \underset{(0.209)}{0.419\, \dot{r}} - \underset{(16.0)}{46.1 \log RNE_{-1}}.$$

$$\bar{R}^2 = 0.66; \text{ Durbin-Watson} = 1.69; \text{ standard error} = 2.28$$

Here $\dot{W}$ is the rate of change in wage per hour for a male adult industrial worker, t is a time trend, u is open unemployment, $\dot{P}$ is the rate of change of the GNP deflator, $\dot{r}$ is the rate of change of the retention ratio (defined as 1 minus the income tax rate), and RNE is real wage income after taxes.

All coefficients have the expected sign, but the labor market variable is not significant. Some experimentation with this equation for various subperiods has shown that its stability cannot be judged satisfactory. Therefore, some additional work is necessary before firm conclusions are drawn on Swedish conditions. Preliminary results from this project, which was carried out with the assistance of Karl Gustav Hansson, are reported in Göran Normann, "Skatter och inflation" (Taxes and Inflation), working paper (Industrial Institute for Economic and Social Research, 1980).

Kingdom, expectations of decreases in the retention ratio may increase the rate of wage inflation. Furthermore, the results indicate that a bad performance of real income after taxes may affect the wage change positively. These results therefore seem to imply that increases in the value-added tax and other taxes may well lead to increased wages and thus induce more inflation because of pressure from the cost side.

Economic Effects: Distribution

One empirical study has estimated the distributional effects of the value-added and other taxes in Sweden.[11] This study calculated the effects on the incomes of families of varying size and composition at different positions in the income distribution of replacing various taxes with possible alternatives. The change in real income for each family was measured by the sum of the change in net wages and gross prices paid for goods attributable to the change in taxes. The lump-sum transfer that would just permit families after the tax change to buy the same goods and services with the same amount of work as they could buy before the change is the measure of the effect of the tax change. No effect of tax changes on capital formation or saving is recognized, and the value-added tax is assumed to be fully reflected in consumer prices.

Based on these assumptions, replacement of the 10 percent value-added tax in effect in 1970 with a proportional income tax would *increase* real income for single, childless persons with incomes below 15,000 kronor and for single persons with children and married persons with incomes below 40,000 kronor, all in 1970 prices. It is apparent that value-added tax burdens are regressively distributed relative to burdens of a proportional income tax.[12]

11. Thomas Franzen, Kerstin Lövgren, and Irma Rosenberg, "Redistributional Effects of Taxes and Public Expenditures in Sweden," *Swedish Journal of Economics,* vol. 77, no. 1 (1975), pp. 31–55.

12. Franzen, Lövgren, and Rosenberg, ibid., also estimated the effects of replacing payroll taxes, existing income taxes, and all taxes with a proportional income tax. They found that an income tax would fall less heavily than payroll taxes on the middle ranges of the income distribution but would tax more heavily those at the bottom and top of the distribution. A proportional income tax would substantially increase tax burdens at the bottom and lower middle ranges of the distribution over those under the prevailing income taxes and would substantially reduce tax burdens on upper middle and upper income brackets. The effect of replacing all taxes with a proportional income tax was similar to that of replacing existing income taxes, but the effects were less pronounced. See also Thomas Franzen, Kerstin Lövgren, and Irma Rosenberg, *Skatters och offentliga utgifters effekter pa inkomstfordelningen,* vols. 1 and 2 (Stockholm: Gotab, 1976).

Current Issues

The Social Democratic party, now in opposition, and dominant elements of the trade unions are supporting a modification in the value-added tax to broaden the base from consumption to net national product. It is alleged that including investment would offset the failure to include capital income under the payroll tax and that the broader base would increase the usefulness of the value-added tax as an automatic stabilizer during business cycles. If this change should be adopted, some believe a shift from the destination to the origin principle would be desirable to encourage declines in factor prices. A government commission is examining the practicability and the probable effects of such a change.

Two aspects of the shift in the value-added tax base are dubious. First, the shift from the destination to the origin principle would not necessarily convert increases in prices to decreases in factor payments. The evidence cited above suggests that workers key their demands for increases in money wages to changes in real after-tax incomes. If this finding is correct, their behavior would not be affected by the particular rule adopted for administering the value-added tax. On the other hand, if negotiations can induce workers to accept payroll tax increases and reduce their wage demands in exchange for cuts in income taxes (as the history of the 1970s is interpreted by some), it is unclear why workers could not also be induced to accept an increase in a consumption-based value-added tax instead of an increase in payroll taxes. Second, the argument that the workers necessarily will be spared tax burdens if investment goods are included in the base is shaky. To the extent that any increase in tax collections is reflected in prices, the burden should be much the same as that under a consumption-based tax. However, it is more likely that in a small open economy like that of Sweden a tax on investment goods or capital income will eventually be borne by labor.[13]

In September 1980 the value-added tax was increased from 17.1 percent to 19 percent to try to curb consumption at a time of acute deterioration in the balance of payments. One aspect of this tax increase sheds light on the political pitfalls of making tax policy. It was widely agreed that restrictive action was necessary; the only question was how to impose the restraints. There was some support for reducing the rate at which

13. These arguments are further explored in Göran Normann, "Om behovet av en allmän produktions factorskatt" (On the Need for a General Tax on Production Factors), *Skattenytt,* vol. 29, no. 3 (1979), pp. 90–99.

food is taxed, possibly to zero, but this proposal was rejected, as it had been many times by previous government commissions. Although the need for some restrictive action was apparent and the Swedish constitution empowers two standing committees to increase taxes when the parliament is not in session (subject to later confirmation by the whole parliament), action was deferred. Instead, a special session of parliament had to be called. This happened as a result of the highly unstable political situation in which a three-party coalition in government had a one-vote majority in parliament. Enactment of the tax increase was thus delayed for several weeks, during which there was a rush to buy consumer durable goods.

RICHARD HEMMING *and* JOHN A. KAY

The United Kingdom

ON APRIL 1, 1973, the value-added tax was introduced in Britain, replacing the purchase tax, a single-stage consumption tax charged at the wholesale stage, and the selective employment tax, a payroll tax principally on services. Sales taxes were not, of course, an innovation in the 1970s. Had it not been for excessive taxes on tea two centuries before, April 1973 might also have seen the introduction of the value-added tax in North America.

This paper sketches the background of the value-added tax; its adoption; its rates and structure; its effects on prices, the balance of payments, resource allocation, and distribution; and the costs and problems of administration.

History

The base of the purchase tax and the selective employment tax, taken together, differed only slightly from that of the value-added tax. The purchase tax was imposed on consumer goods and collected from about 74,000 registered businesses. The tax was levied on the wholesale value of specified physical commodities whenever they were sold by a registered business to someone not registered. The principal exceptions were food, fuel, and a few other goods. Certain commodities, such as stationery, furniture, and automobiles, purchased both as final and as intermediate goods were taxed whatever their use or the identity of their purchaser. Tax rates were elaborately differentiated according to political perceptions of how luxurious the commodity was, and the rates were changed frequently. At the time the purchase tax was abolished, three different rates were used to distinguish in a rough way between essentials and luxuries.[1] This distinction survived into the era of the value-added tax. In the last year of its existence the purchase tax yielded 9 percent of total revenue, about 22 percent of the yield of the personal income tax. Because the taxpayers were relatively few and large, administrative costs were low—less than 1 percent of revenue—and compliance costs for taxpayers were probably relatively low as well.

The purchase tax excluded services, which were the province of the selective employment tax, a per capita tax on all employees, collected as a surcharge on social security contributions, and refunded to employers who fell into certain categories (such as local authorities, manufacturing, or farming). The selective employment tax was unpopular to a degree not fully explicable by its failings. Dislike of this tax caused it to serve a function like that of the cascade taxes in France and Germany, from whose faults the value-added tax was intended to bring deliverance.

The value-added tax was first discussed in the United Kingdom in the early 1960s as a possible substitute for all or part of the corporation income tax as a way of encouraging investments and assisting exports. Interest in the new tax subsided after a committee of inquiry heard from leading industrialists that investment was insensitive to capital costs (which disposed of the first argument for the value-added tax) and that they would shift the value-added tax forward into prices though they did not do so for the corporation tax (which disposed of the second argument). The Conservative government elected in 1970 expressed interest in the value-added tax, partly for its own merits and partly because Britain would have to adopt the tax if its application to the European Economic Community were accepted. A 1971 Green Paper proposed that the value-added tax replace both the purchase tax and the selective employment tax in 1973.[2]

The principal arguments against the purchase tax concerned the excessive differentiation of the tax rate structure and the narrowness of the range of goods to which the tax was applied. This case is hard to under-

1. To illustrate the complexity of the rates, silverware and fur coats were taxed at the maximum rate; household textiles were subject to the minimum rate after having been tax-free for many years; such relatively unessential items as ice cream and chocolate biscuits were taxed, but luxury items such as smoked salmon and caviar were exempt along with such unglamorous items as smoked cod and cod roe.

2. *Value-Added Tax*, Green Paper, Presented to the Parliament by the Chancellor of the Exchequer by Command of Her Majesty (London: Her Majesty's Stationery Office, 1971).

stand, as it is possible to levy either the value-added tax or the purchase tax on as wide or as narrow a range of goods as desired. As it turned out, the range of goods subject to the standard value-added tax rate was almost identical to that subject to the purchase tax. The standard rate applied also to certain goods previously subject to excise taxes only; but as the excises were reduced by compensating amounts, this change had little practical significance.

A subsidiary group of arguments claimed balance-of-payments advantages from the switch. There was no direct impact, as the purchase tax was not levied on exports, although it was levied on such commodities as stationery and furniture that entered the cost of exports, and rebates would be automatic under the value-added tax. In any event, the pound was allowed to float in June 1972, depriving this argument of any relevance.

As introduction of the value-added tax neared, debate over its desirability subsided. In 1972, a year after the intention to introduce the tax was announced and a year before it was implemented, the government announced that a single rate of 10 percent would apply to all goods not zero rated, and Parliament began to consider legislation. In August 1972 registration of traders for tax purposes began, together with an information campaign. The 1973 budget confirmed the 10 percent rate and slightly narrowed the base a few days before implementation.

Structure

The British value-added tax is typical of the European species—it is collected at all stages of production according to the invoice system and on the destination principle. It conforms to the requirements of the sixth directive of the European Economic Community, issued in 1977.

There are three classes of goods and services for tax purposes. The largest is subject to the standard rate, now 15 percent of value exclusive of tax. Exports and a variety of goods and services that the government wishes to free from tax on social and political grounds are zero rated. A third category of goods is tax exempt. From 1975 to 1979 certain "non-essential" goods were subject to a higher than normal rate.[3]

A taxable person is a supplier who in the course of business makes taxable supplies whose value exceeds the registration limit, now £13,500

3. See the appendix to this paper for a listing of some of the goods in each category.

a year. Business whose sales are less than £13,500 may elect to be taxable if it is to their advantage. Once registered, a taxpayer must remain registered for two years; if sales fall below £12,500, a taxpayer may apply for deregistration. The number of registered taxpayers rose gradually from 1,196,700 in 1974 to 1,292,300 in 1979.[4]

The standard tax period is three months although firms regularly claiming refunds may use shorter periods. No specific accounting procedure is laid down; however, simplified schemes for calculating liability have been designed for retailers and partially exempt traders. Nine special schemes have also been designed to aid certain retailers that have many transactions of low unit value, do not normally issue invoices, and trade in goods subject to different rates of tax. Other special rules apply to businesses that must allocate expenses because some of the goods they sell are taxable while others are exempt.

The value-added tax has undergone a number of changes since its introduction in 1973. The standard rate has been changed; the luxury rate was introduced, reduced, and abolished. Registration and deregistration limits have been raised (see the appendix). Some of the changes have had regulatory objectives. The reduction in the standard rate from 10 to 8 percent in July 1974 was designed to slow inflation by reducing indexed wage adjustments. The 25 percent rate on gasoline introduced in November 1974 was intended to reduce demand more than the OPEC price rise alone would have done; five months later the same rate was extended to a wide range of "nonessential" goods. A year later the luxury rate was cut in half because it was blamed for difficulties faced by the British electrical industry. The Conservative government in 1979 replaced the 8 percent standard rate and the luxury rate of 12.5 percent by a single rate of 15 percent.

The value-added tax base closely resembles that of the purchase tax. No more than 2 percent of consumer expenditure is devoted to goods (such as brushes, brooms, mops, pianos, school satchels, and toilet paper) subject to the value-added tax but not previously to the purchase tax or excise duties. About 10 percent of consumer expenditure is on services within the tax base for the value-added tax. Value-added tax is imposed on alcoholic drinks and tobacco, but compensating reductions in the previously existing excises were allowed. There is no substance to the

4. Commissioners of Her Majesty's Customs and Excise, *Reports* (HMSO, selected issues, 1975–80).

Table 1. Household Expenditure Subject to the Value-Added Tax, 1977
Pounds per week

Expenditure category	*Exempt*	*Zero*	*Rate* 8 *percent*	12.5 *percent*	*Total*
Housing	8.86	0.49	1.41	0	10.76
Fuel, light, and power	0	4.38	0	0	4.38
Food	0	14.68	3.06	0	17.74
Drink	0	0	6.18	0	6.18
Tobacco	0	0	3.46	0	3.46
Clothing and footwear	0	0.78	5.00	0	5.78
Desirables	0	0	3.42	1.57	4.99
Other goods	0	1.52	3.97	0.40	5.89
Transport and vehicles	0.90	1.70	4.69	2.42	9.71
Services	1.06	0.08	5.79	0	6.93
Total	10.82	23.63	36.98	4.39	75.82
With annual income of £3,000	6.86	23.29	26.54	3.39	60.08
With annual income of £10,000	10.77	28.74	57.34	7.02	103.87

Source: Authors' tabulations from unpublished Family Expenditure Survey data.

claim made in the 1971 Green Paper that the value-added tax would broaden the base of indirect taxation in the United Kingdom. Table 1 shows that just over half of consumption expenditure is subject to positive rates of the value-added tax. The principal reason for the narrowness of the base is concern about the distributional impact of the tax.

Perhaps the most arbitrary distinction in value-added tax coverage, and certainly the one most productive of dispute, is that made between new construction, which is zero rated, and building repair and maintenance, which is standard rated.[5] Such a distinction clearly produces significant economic distortion; however, directives of the EEC preclude the extension of zero rates, while the extension of the standard rate to

5. Editor's note: During the conference discussion, Alan Prest reported on a judicial case in which the issue was whether the construction of a new foundation under an existing building should be regarded as new construction (which is zero rated) or a repair (which is fully taxable). The trial court ruled that the work was in the nature of a repair and therefore fully taxable. On appeal, it was ruled that the work was new construction and therefore zero rated. The court of appeals, presided over by Lord Denning, perhaps the most distinguished British judge of the twentieth century, next heard the case. Responding to the question of how the work could in any sense be characterized as an extension of the building and hence zero rated, Lord Denning said that to supply new foundations was an extension of a building "in a downward direction" and therefore zero rated.

construction would imply a large uncovenanted transfer from prospective to present owners of housing.

Effects of the Tax

The value-added tax has had fewer economic effects—on investment, on the balance of payments, and on the distribution of taxes—than its supporters claimed or its opponents feared. This section outlines the evidence about the impact of the value-added tax in each of these areas.

Effective Rates

One of the attractions of the value-added tax is that it can be levied at the same rate on all consumer goods (except leisure), thus leaving the relative price of taxed goods unchanged. The inability to tax leisure does, of course, destroy the theoretical argument for the necessary superiority of the value-added tax, but there are reasons, both theoretical and practical, for supposing that the costs of extensive discrimination in rates of tax on different commodities will exceed the benefits.

It is important, therefore, to note that as soon as any complication in rate structure is introduced, the pattern of uniformity flies apart completely. For example, most food is zero rated in Britain, but restaurant meals are taxed at 15 percent. Because the 15 percent rate is applied to the whole value of the output while there is no input tax to be refunded on the food content of inputs, the value added in catering is taxed at a much higher rate than 15 percent.[6] Table 2 presents estimates of the effective rate of the value-added tax on selected input-output industries in the United Kingdom. The range of effective rates, from −24.3 percent to 37 percent, is far broader than the range of nominal rates. It is important to note that these differences in effective rates affect decisions by individual consumers about whether to buy a particular commodity or produce

6. If a_{ij} represents the requirement from industry i per unit of output of industry j, and t_j is the nominal rate on the output of industry j, then the effective tax rate on value added in industry j is $t_j = (t_j - \sum_i a_{ij} t_i)/(1 - a_{ij})$. See John A. Kay and Neil A. Warren, "Effective Rates of Value Added Tax," working paper (London: Institute for Fiscal Studies, 1980). There is an analogy between the effective rate of value-added tax and the effective rate of protection in international trade; see W. M. Corden, *The Theory of Protection* (London: Oxford University Press, 1971), chap. 3.

Table 2. Nominal and Effective Rates of the Value-Added Tax, 1980
Percent

Commodity group	Nominal rate	Effective rate	Consumer expenditure: As percent of final demand	Consumer expenditure: Distribution
Agriculture	0	−5.6	93.0	6.3
Cereal products	0	−13.3	91.8	3.8
Sugar, cocoa, etc.	0	−12.6	80.2	2.0
Other food products[a]	0	−24.3	87.7	12.9
Alcoholic drinks	15	16.3	69.8	8.6
Tobacco	15	27.8	88.6	5.4
Iron and steel[b]	15	31.3	0.0	0.0
Motor vehicles	15	17.7	24.1	4.1
Leather, leather goods, and furs	15	37.0	40.4	0.5
Building materials	15	26.7	28.9	0.6
Construction	0	−7.3	14.2	3.0
Electricity	0	−4.3	84.1	2.6
Distributive trades	15	18.9	85.9	1.2
Miscellaneous services	15	17.0	54.2	10.4

Source: John A. Kay and Neil A. Warren, "Effective Rates of Value Added Tax," working paper (London: Institute for Fiscal Studies, 1980).
a. Not including preceding items and oils and fats.
b. Not including iron castings.

it themselves, and in some cases there is no real option. Effective rates do not, in general, represent the rates that businesses would face in deciding whether to produce a good themselves or to obtain it from another supplier.

Nevertheless, the dispersion of effective rates creates distortions beyond those explicitly intended. A customer of a British branch of McDonald's is offered two prices depending on whether he wishes to take his hamburger away (buy food, a zero-rated transaction) or eat it on the premises (consume a restaurant meal and pay value-added tax at the standard rate). It is probably not entirely coincidental that the Westminster branch of McDonald's has chosen a location immediately adjacent to the piazza of Westminster Cathedral.

Prices and the Balance of Payments

The National Institute of Economic and Social Research (NIESR) tried to estimate the effect that introducing the value-added tax would have on the retail price index,[7] on the assumptions that the new tax would be fully shifted to consumers, that its full potential yield would be realized, and that its nominal rates would equal the effective rate on all goods. Depending on the assumptions made about the shifting of the selective employment tax and the offsetting adjustments in excises, the retail price index was expected to change by −0.25 to +2.5 percent. By August 1973 prices had risen by about 2.5 percent, and by December 1973, by 8 percent. How much of the increase in prices should be attributed to the introduction of the value-added tax is far from clear.

The effect on prices of the 1979 increases in the value-added tax may have been more important. The direct impact of the increase in the standard rate of 8 percent and the luxury rate of 12.5 percent to a single rate of 15 percent was an increase in the price level officially estimated at 3.75 percent. It seems probable that this increase contributed to an increase in inflationary expectations that magnified the direct effect. In the year ending in June 1979 retail prices rose by 11.4 percent; in the subsequent twelve months (to June 1980) retail prices jumped 20.8 percent.

The balance-of-payments effects of replacing the purchase tax and the selective employment tax with the value-added tax were expected to be negligible, according to the NIESR study. Because exports were not subject to the purchase tax, the effect could not be great. Some exported services did bear the selective employment tax while under the value-added tax some exported services were zero rated, but the effect of this change was expected to be minor. All in all, exports were expected to increase by about 0.25 percent from the tax switch.

Investment

Discussion of the possible stimulation of investment relates to substituting the value-added tax for the personal or the corporation income tax. Because the value-added tax replaced sales taxes in the United Kingdom, no significant effects should be anticipated, certainly not in comparison with other events such as the introduction of the imputation system of corporation income tax and expensing of investments in plant and machinery. Because there is some evidence that the selective employment tax

7. National Institute of Economic and Social Research, "The Economic Situation: Chapter 1, The Home Economy," *National Institute Economic Review*, no. 60 (May 1972), pp. 16–21.

did increase the capital-intensiveness of services,[8] its abolition may have led to some decrease.

Distributional Effects

As in other countries, the distributional effects of the value-added tax were a major issue in the United Kingdom. Most taxpayers in the United Kingdom face what amounts to a linear tax schedule. The first £11,250 of taxable income is charged at the basic rate of 30 percent, and only 3 percent of tax units have taxable income above this amount. Sixty percent of all tax revenue comes from the basic portion of the income tax and from the proportional social security tax.

In general, a linear tax of the form $t = by - a$ (where t is tax, y is income, and a and b are parameters) is progressive if a is positive and regressive if a is negative. If the schedules (a_1, b_1) and (a_2, b_2) yield equal revenue, the first schedule is more progressive if $b_1 > b_2$ and (as a necessary implication of the equal yield condition) $a_1 > a_2$. Thus examination of the parameters of the linearized schedule permits conclusions about progressivity.[9]

Table 3 contains estimates of a and b for four groups of taxes for three types of taxpayers. The burdens of the value-added tax are computed relative to income before income tax.[10] It is also possible to define the

8. W. B. Reddaway, *Effects of the Selective Employment Tax: First Report, The Distributive Trades* (HMSO, 1970), pp. 129–32.

9. See Richard Hemming, "Income Tax Progressivity and Labor Supply," *Journal of Public Economics,* vol. 14 (August 1980), pp. 95–100. There are numerous ways to measure tax progressivity. Some consider the impact of taxes on income inequality via the Lorenz curve; others examine the properties of the distribution of tax payments directly.

10. The division of liability between interacting taxes is somewhat arbitrary. If a tax is levied on income, y, on a schedule $c_0y - d_0$, and value-added tax is levied on expenditure, e, according to an equation $c_1e - d_1$ (where the subscript 0 denotes the income tax and the subscript 1 denotes the value-added tax), and if there are no savings, then tax paid is $(c_0 + c_1 - c_1c_0)y - (d_0 + d_1 - c_1d_0)$. In table 3, we have set $b_0 = c_0$, $b_1 = c_1 - c_1c_0$, $a_0 = d_0$, and $a_1 = d_1 - c_1d_0$, so that the income tax data reflect the actual legislated schedule as modified by income-related allowances. This procedure implies that if $d_1 = 0$, then $a_1 > 0$, because c_1 and d_0 exceed zero; as a result, a proportional value-added tax would appear regressive, reflecting the fact that expenditure rises less than proportionately with gross income under a progressive income tax.

Table 3. The Distributional Impact of the Tax System, 1980–81

Tax credits in pounds; rates in percent

	Single person		*Married couple, one earner*		*Married couple, two earners*	
Tax	*Tax credit* $(-a_i)$	*Marginal rate* (b_i)	*Tax credit* $(-a_i)$	*Marginal rate* (b_i)	*Tax credit* $(-a_i)$	*Marginal rate* (b_i)
Income	355	0.241	618	0.242	966	0.238
Social security	...	0.179	...	0.179	...	0.179
Value-added	84	0.060	66	0.056	45	0.062
Other indirect	12	0.103	−209	0.076	−219	0.080
Total	451	0.583	475	0.553	792	0.559

Source: C. N. Morris, "The Impact of the 1980 Budget," *Fiscal Studies*, vol. 1 (July 1980), pp. 45–46.

progressivity of the value-added tax relative to income after income tax.[11] Table 3 shows that even measured against gross income, the British value-added tax is progressive, in contrast with other indirect taxes, which are regressive (largely because of tobacco duties). The progressivity of the value-added tax is a consequence of zero rating. A four-person family earning £3,000 pays the standard rate on 42.6 percent of its expenditure; for one earning £10,000 this figure is 53.7 percent (see table 1).

The major shift from income tax to value-added tax in 1979 increased the progressivity of the British tax system. As a result of the replacement of the 8 and 12.5 percent rates by the single 15 percent rate, the equation describing the relation of value-added tax payments, t, to expenditures, e, changed from $t = 0.0635e - 78$ to $t = 0.1127e - 130$.[12] With a prebudget income tax rate of 33 percent, the new income tax rate that would have left overall distribution unaffected would have been 29.5 percent. In fact, the basic rate was lowered only to 30 percent, and the balance of

11. This view, adopted by Edgar K. Browning and William R. Johnson, *The Distribution of the Tax Burden* (Washington, D.C.: American Enterprise Institute for Public Policy Research, 1979), has some plausibility since the income tax threshold in Britain is indexed, and the increase in value-added tax in 1979 did result in an increase in the tax threshold when indexation of the threshold took place in the next budget. Under this procedure, $a_0 = (1 - c_1)d_0$ and $a_1 = d_1$; value-added tax payments would be proportional to gross income and income tax would be less progressive than the legislated schedule suggests. In general, the Browning and Johnson procedure would show income tax as less progressive and indirect taxes such as the value-added tax as more progressive than under our methods; the choice does not affect the progressivity of the tax and benefit system taken as a whole.

12. See J. A. Kay and C. N. Morris, "Direct and Indirect Taxes: Some Effects of the 1979 Budget," *Fiscal Studies*, vol. 1 (November 1979), pp. 1–10.

revenue was used to increase the income tax threshold.[13] In view of this result, both the Conservative government's claim that the 1979 budget improved incentives and the Labour opposition's criticism of its regressive impact seem misplaced.

Zero rating is responsible for the progressivity of the value-added tax, but it narrows the tax and causes distortions. It would be possible to reproduce the distributional effects of the present system if zero rating was abolished and the following simple changes in the income tax were made: the basic rate would be reduced by 0.775 percentage point, and the income tax threshold of single persons and couples would be raised by £259 and £423, respectively.[14] There would be little change in progressivity if zero rating was abolished and the revenue used to cut one point from the basic rate of income tax with the balance used to increase the tax threshold.

In summary, the value-added tax in the United Kingdom is progressive, the recent shift to increased value-added taxation with reduced and modified personal income taxation has increased progressivity mildly, and a broad-based value-added tax together with simple changes in the income tax could reproduce the present distribution of burdens in the aggregate. These observations suggest strongly that it is inappropriate to make general statements about the distributional impact of the value-added tax except in the context of the whole tax system of which it forms a part.

Operating Costs

The costs of the value-added tax consist of administrative costs imposed on the government and compliance costs borne directly by taxpayers.[15]

13. From footnote 10, it is apparent that neutrality of the tax shift with revenue held constant requires that $(c_0 + c_1 - c_1c_0)$ remain constant. In fact, it increased slightly, indicating increased progressivity.

14. These estimates are drawn from J. A. Kay and M. A. King, *The British Tax System* (London: Oxford University Press, 1978), pp. 244–45. The change in revenue from zero rating is:

$$VAT = 77.8 + \underset{(4.2)}{49.1\,D} - \underset{(0.087)}{0.775\,Y},$$
$$R^2 = 0.962$$

where *VAT* is the loss in value-added tax from zero rating in pounds per year in 1979 prices, *D* is a dummy variable for a two-person household, and *Y* is income.

15. Cedric Sandford, "Tax Compliance Costs Matter: Chancellor Please Note," *British Tax Review*, no. 4 (1976), pp. 205–12.

The value-added tax is administered by Her Majesty's Customs and Excises, along with other indirect taxes, and is not integrated with direct taxation. To administer the tax, new machinery had to be created. Value-added tax records were fully computerized from the outset; this is in stark contrast to the administration of direct taxes, in particular the income tax, the Inland Revenue having not yet found it possible to use computers to ease its work load.[16]

The need to establish new administrative machinery and the twenty-fold increase in the number of registrations for the value-added tax over those for the purchase tax were expected to raise administrative costs, and these expectations were borne out. From 1975 through 1979 value-added tax administrative costs averaged just over 2 percent of collections, compared with 0.75 percent under the purchase tax.[17] With the sharp increase in rates in 1979, administrative costs as a percentage of collections dropped to about 1.25 percent. The value-added tax costs about as much to administer per pound of revenue as taxes administered by the Inland Revenue (whose ratio of administrative costs to yield is roughly four times that of the U.S. Internal Revenue Service), much less than protective duties, which cost about 4.5 percent of revenue to collect, but much more than tobacco duties, which cost only 0.1 percent of revenue to collect.

Because the value-added tax is self-assessed, compliance costs borne by taxpayers are part of the collection cost. For large firms, such costs are small in relation to tax paid, but for small firms and especially for those unsure whether or not to register, the costs are proportionately much greater because some of the costs are one time only while others rise far less quickly with the size of the firm than revenues do.

Some work on measuring compliance costs has been undertaken by Godwin and Sandford. Godwin estimated that the average costs of compliance among twenty-nine small traders was 78 percent of net revenue.[18] Even excluding seven druggists who claimed refunds, compliance costs were 31 percent of revenue. Measuring compliance costs against turnover, not revenue, Sandford found that the mean compliance costs among

16. The suitability of the various sites available to Customs and Excise for housing a major computer installation was the major factor in determining the location of the central administrative unit for the value-added tax at Southend-on-Sea, some forty miles from London. D. Johnstone, *A Tax Shall Be Charged* (HMSO, 1975).

17. See Commissioners of Her Majesty's Customs and Excise, *Reports* (HMSO, selected issues, 1975–80).

18. M. Godwin, "VAT: Compliance Costs to the Independent Retailer," *Accountancy* (September 1976), pp. 48–60.

eighty-nine firms of different sizes was 0.37 percent for firms taxed at a single rate and 0.87 percent for firms with multiple-rated output; considerable economies of scale in compliance were found, and the costs borne by the quartile of firms with the largest turnover were five times those of the quartile of firms with the lowest turnover.[19]

The built-in policing that the invoice method is claimed to provide is illusory. Even on transactions between registered traders, a buyer has an incentive to ensure that an invoice is issued but none to ensure that tax is indeed paid. Such checks could only be made by first tracing all invoices issued by a trader when corresponding claims for repayment of input tax were made by any of the other 1.25 million registered taxpayers, and then matching the totals of these to that trader's declared output, a task that is clearly impossible. In practice, compliance is imposed by random checks of accounting procedures.

Nevertheless compliance is high, with revenue loss from evasion about 1.5 percent of potential revenue. This estimate is based on the additional revenue obtained from a selection of cases subjected to intensive inquiry. Certain civil service trade unions believe that true evasion is more than three times as great, but there are obvious reasons why this estimate is likely to be high. The precise extent of value-added tax fraud is not, and probably never will be, known.

Conclusions

We think that the value-added tax in Britain has few advantages over the taxes it replaced and would not have been adopted but for the requirements of the EEC. It is not surprising, therefore, that the British version closely follows the European norm, except for the wide range of goods that are zero rated and the relatively high threshold for registration. The first feature is explained by the effort of those who designed the value-added tax to reproduce as closely as possible the taxes that preceded it. The second feature is explained by the unusually small fraction of economic activity handled by small businesses in Britain.

What lessons does the British experience hold for a country contemplating the adoption of the value-added tax? One is that a value-added tax

19. C. T. Sandford and others, "Some Preliminary Findings on the Compliance Costs of VAT: Report of a Pilot Study," Occasional Paper 7 (Bath University, Center for Fiscal Studies, 1979). A more detailed study of compliance costs and other aspects of value-added tax administration has recently been published; C. T. Sandford and others, *Costs and Benefits of VAT* (London: Heinemann, 1981).

that can be implemented is bound to fall well short of the theoretical ideal; there are some difficulties in applying the full value-added tax principle to retailing and greater difficulties in applying it to the financial sector, for example. The second lesson is that the value-added tax need not be a regressive tax if one is willing to bear the administrative complications and economic distortions that zero rates and exemptions generate. It is better, we believe, to pursue distributional objectives with other instruments.

Appendix

Commodities Subject to Zero Rate Schedule[20]

Food (except certain nonessential foodstuffs, alcoholic and soft drinks, pet food, and food supplied by caterers); sewerage services and water; books, newspapers, and maps; talking books for the blind and handicapped and radios for the blind; newspaper advertisements; news services; fuel and power (except fuel for vehicles); construction of buildings (but not repair and maintenance); international services; transport (major exclusions are boats and aircraft used for recreational purposes, car parking, unaccompanied vehicles and luggage, and freight movements wholly within the United Kingdom); large trailers and houseboats; gold dealing; bank notes; prescription drugs and medicines, medical and surgical appliances; exports; charities (only the sale of goods donated by individuals); children's clothing and footwear; protective boots and helmets for industrial use and crash helmets.

Exempt Commodities[21]

Land; insurance; postal services; betting, gaming, and lotteries; finance; education; health; burial and cremation; trade unions and professional bodies.

Commodities Subject to Higher Rate[22]

Electrical domestic appliances (but not stoves and heaters); radio and television sets; pleasure boats and light aircraft; touring trailers; photo-

20. Her Majesty's Customs and Excise, *Value-Added Tax: Scope and Coverage*, Notice 701 (McCorquodale for HMSO, 1979).

21. Ibid.

22. Operative May 1, 1975, to June 18, 1979; Her Majesty's Customs and Excise, *Value-Added Tax: Scope and Coverage*, Notice 701 (McCorquodale for HMSO, 1976).

graphic equipment and binoculars; furs; jewelry; goldsmiths' and silversmiths' wares; gasoline.

Calendar of Value-Added Tax Events in the United Kingdom

June 18, 1970	Conservative government elected. Its manifesto contained a promise to abolish the selective employment tax and investigate the possibility of introducing the value-added tax.
March 30, 1971	Green Paper published; budget announcement that the value-added tax is to be introduced in April 1973, to replace the selective employment and purchase taxes.
March 21, 1972	White Paper published.
August 1972	Public notices published.
March 6, 1973	10 percent standard rate of the value-added tax announced in budget.
April 1, 1973	Value-added taxation commences.
April 1, 1974	Coverage of the value-added tax extended in budget to gasoline, vehicle fuels, and certain categories of food and drink.
July 29, 1974	Standard rate of the value-added tax reduced in minibudget to 8 percent.
November 18, 1974	Rate of the value-added tax on gasoline raised in minibudget to 25 percent.
May 1, 1975	25 percent rate extended to a range of less essential goods.
April 12, 1976	Higher rate of the value-added tax reduced in budget to 12.5 percent.
October 1, 1977	Registration limit raised from £5,000 to £7,500 and deregistration limit from £4,000 to £6,000.
April 12, 1978	Registration limit raised in budget to £10,000 and deregistration limit to £8,500.
June 18, 1979	Standard and higher rates replaced by a single rate of 15 percent.
March 27, 1980	Registration limit raised in budget to £13,500 and deregistration limit to £12,500.
June 1, 1980	Lubricating oils standard-rated.

DIETER POHMER

Germany

THE PROCESS leading to the adoption of the value-added tax in Germany began more than sixty years ago. In 1918 Germany converted a stamp sales tax into an all-stage gross turnover tax to help pay for the war. Within a year the industrialist Carl Friedrich von Siemens spoke in the Reichstag on behalf of a "refined turnover tax," or, in today's parlance, a value-added tax of the income type. Many industrialists, notably in small business, began to criticize the turnover tax on the ground that it created incentives for firms to integrate vertically to avoid part of the tax.

Despite continued criticism from businessmen and others, the all-stage gross turnover tax lasted half a century. In the 1950s widespread discussion began on how to reform the gross turnover tax, but these efforts bore fruit only in 1968.[1]

The Federal Constitutional Court handed down a decision on December 20, 1966, placing "temporal limits" on the "further validity of the turnover tax." On April 11, 1967, the Council of the European Economic

1. As illustrations of this discussion, see Wissenschaftlicher Beirat beim Bundesministerium der Finanzen (Scientific Advisory of the Federal Finance Ministry), *Organische Steuerreform* (Organic Tax Reform), Bylaw to the Federal Finance Ministry (Bonn: Bundesministerium der Finanzen, 1953); Günther Schmölders, *Organische Steuerreform, Grundlagen, Vorarbeiten, Gesetzentwürfe* (Organic Tax Reform, Bases, Preparations, Law Proposals) (Berlin and Frankfurt am Main: Franz Vahlen, 1953); Hans Ritschl, *Die Grosse Steuerreform* (The Big Tax Reform), *Gutachten* (expert opinion) (Hamburg, 1953); Dieter Pohmer, *Die Neuordnung der Umsatzbesteuerung, Grundlagen der Bisherigen Diskussion und Grundsätze einer Reform* (The Reform of the Turnover Tax, Bases of the Previous Dicussion and Bases of a Reform) (Bonn: Unternehmerwirtschaft-Verlags Ambtt, 1960).

Community handed down its first directive requiring members of the Community to introduce value-added taxes.

This paper describes the adoption of the tax in Germany, its structure, attitudes toward it, administrative problems and issues, and its effects on prices, saving, income distribution, and international trade.

Introduction of the Tax

The value-added tax was introduced to reform the tax structure, not to increase tax revenues; to end the baneful effects of the gross turnover tax; and above all to bring general consumer taxation into line with that of other members of the European Economic Community.

Adoption

As early as 1963 the federal government sent the Fourth Bundestag a "Blueprint for a Turnover Tax Law," which envisaged an income-type value-added tax based on the accounts method. The proposal was debated carefully for two years but not enacted. It was reintroduced in 1965 by the Christian Democratic/Christian Social party in coalition with the Free Democratic party. Further deliberation and public hearings led to important modifications, and on May 29, 1967, a consumption-type value-added tax collected by the invoice method was enacted, to become effective January 1, 1968. The decision to adopt the invoice method rather than the accounts method was more in harmony with directives of the EEC. Requests from pressure groups for tax exemptions are politically more difficult because in these cases a "cancel-out effect" on subsequent production stages is usually caused by a decrease in the prepaid tax.

The weightiest arguments on behalf of the new law, as mentioned above, were the need to harmonize taxes within the EEC and the desire to eliminate perverse incentives within the gross turnover tax. The turnover tax had also grown complex, in part because of efforts to reduce the incentives for vertical integration; effective tax rates differed across classes of commodities according to how frequently they were bought and sold before reaching final consumers. Border adjustments were hard to make.

Some opponents of the new tax alleged that the incentives for vertical integration under the turnover tax were less serious than proponents held; paradoxically, others were loath to lose competitive advantages they enjoyed because they had integrated vertically. Some opponents held that the new tax would impose needless administrative burdens on small businesses.

Structure

The German value-added tax closely resembles that of other members of the European Economic Community. It is imposed on all sales (including appropriation for own use) by all businesses except those explicitly exempted. The selection of the consumption base means that taxes paid by their suppliers may be deducted in computing their liability; therefore investment goods are tax free. Exports are zero rated. Some banking and finance transactions, as well as sales of land and comparable activities that are subject to special taxes, are tax exempt.

The value-added tax is imposed at two rates—a normal rate and a preferential rate. When the value-added tax was introduced, the normal rate was 10 percent. Six months later the normal rate was increased to 11 percent. On January 1, 1978, the normal rate was raised to 12 percent, and on July 1, 1979, to 13 percent. In each case the preferential rate was set at one-half of the normal rate. The preferential rate applies to certain foods, animals, plants and some agricultural products, books, and newspapers.

The German value-added tax contains a large number of exemptions, particularly for health, education, and social purposes. All taxable businesses, whether subject to the normal, reduced, or zero rate, may deduct any taxes paid by suppliers (including taxes on imports) in computing liability and are entitled to a refund if these deductions exceed their liability. Firms, however, are not entitled to take such deductions on exempt transactions. In these cases exemption may increase the tax load rather than reduce it. This paradox can result if intermediate stages of production are exempt when both earlier and later stages are taxable, because value added in the earlier stages is taxed twice. For this reason, firms with exempt transactions may, in certain cases, waive this thoroughly mixed blessing and make themselves taxable. It would be better if the exempt classification was dropped and firms that the government wishes to tax more lightly than others were given concessionary rates.

In general, the value-added tax liability dates from the time a bill is submitted, but in some cases firms are taxed only when payment is actually made. This provision makes compliance easier for small businesses, but other provisions designed to reduce burdens for small businesses are questionable. Annual sales of 20,000 deutsche marks or less are exempt. This procedure may increase the effective rate of taxation on goods produced by small businesses for the same reason that other tax exemptions may have this effect. Firms with sales of up to 60,000 deutsche marks are subject to the value-added tax, but they are allowed some relief based on sales. This regulation is unjustified because firms report more taxes on purchases than they have actually paid.

The taxation of sales to government is also unjustifiable as this procedure violates the principle of taxing consumption.

The German value-added tax has not always fallen exclusively on consumption. In 1967 a temporary tax was imposed on investment to discourage businesses from deferring investment until the value-added tax, which exempted investment, replaced the gross turnover tax, which taxed investment. On one other occasion (in the boom of 1973) investment in plant and equipment was taxed for reasons of compensatory fiscal policy, but this tax was canceled only a few months after it was imposed under pressure of the "oil shock." All in all, the value-added tax has been amended more than twenty times, but except for the changes in rates and in the treatment of investment goods, these changes have been relatively minor.

Attitudes

Few people enjoy paying taxes, but the value-added tax has functioned better than even its supporters anticipated. Collection is smooth, in large part because the basic administrative apparatus was already in place to administer the predecessor gross turnover tax. Consumer resistance was negligible because the value-added tax replaced a similar tax and had no immediately perceptible impact on prices. The value-added tax did change relative prices and these changes required a number of adjustments, particularly at the time of transition from the gross turnover tax to the value-added tax. But these problems were quickly resolved, and in a certain sense they should be attributed to the distortions contained in the gross turnover tax rather than to the more neutral value-added tax that replaced it.

A significant problem has arisen concerning used goods. Sales by private households, which are not classified as entrepreneurs, are not taxable; but sales of goods, new or used, by dealers, who are classified as entrepreneurs, are taxable. Dealers in used products are therefore at a disadvantage in competing with direct person-to-person sales. For automobiles, this disadvantage has become severe,[2] but it has also become a problem for traders in other commodities with active secondhand markets, such as furniture, cameras, and television sets, and for such collectible items as gold bars, coins, and stamps. This annoying problem is probably inherent in the value-added tax and any other tax levied at the retail stage.

The attitude of other businesses toward the value-added tax is favorable, except for firms that mourn the lost advantages of vertical integration under the turnover tax. Farmers are effectively freed of the value-added tax burden because of the system of deductions based on gross sales that they are allowed to claim. In contrast to trade unions in some other countries, German unions have acquiesced in the periodic increases in value-added tax and reductions in the income tax. Actually, this shift in the composition of taxes has benefited most workers.

Effects of the Tax

The value-added tax was expected to yield the same amount of revenue as the gross turnover tax that it replaced. Accordingly, direct effects on the general price level were expected to be slight. However, the new tax did change relative prices. To the extent that increases in prices of commodities on which the tax burden increased were more certain than decreases in prices of commodities on which the tax burden decreased, some stimulus to inflation could occur. In fact, prices rose 1.3 percent in the month following the introduction of the value-added tax, two-thirds of which the Deutsche Bundesbank attributed to the tax. This increase was explainable in large part because the value-added tax covered services more broadly than the gross turnover tax had. The

2. See Dieter Pohmer and Franz Xaver Bea, *Die Behandlung gebrauchter Kraftfahrzeuge im deutschen Umsatzsteuerrecht* (The Treatment of Used Automobiles under the German Turnover Tax Law), *Gutachten,* Schriftenreihe des Verbandes der Automobilindustrie, no. 17 (Frankfurt am Main: Verband der Automobilindustrie, 1973).

special transitional tax on investment also bore part of the responsibility for the jump in prices, as did the cancellation of certain exemptions and concessionary rates. The prices of gas and electricity, for example, jumped 9.9 and 6.3 percent, respectively.

The repeated increases in the rate of the value-added tax offer a better chance than the introduction of the tax for studying its price effects. Unfortunately, no econometric study of these effects has been done.[3] This lack also makes it impossible, in principle, to measure the degree to which tax increases indirectly cause price increases greater than the initial impetus as a result of the incorporation of higher prices in wage demands, and higher wages, of course, result in still higher prices. In practice, the last value-added tax increases were paired with cuts in personal income taxes, giving the unions no occasion to justify demands for wage increases by increases in the value-added tax. Even meticulous empirical analysis would have had a hard time untangling the effects of 1 percent step-ups in the value-added tax rate against the background of inflation several times greater.[4]

There is no adequate empirical study of the effects of the value-added tax on consumption and saving in Germany. It is possible to compare the rates of saving in recent years, during which value-added taxes remained constant, with those in years when rates were increased, but these comparisons are not very instructive. Nevertheless, the fact that savings grew faster than consumption during 1979, when value-added tax rates also rose, but grew more slowly during 1976 and 1977, when rates were stable, does accord with the view that the value-added tax encourages saving. The year 1978 is hard to classify: consumption and saving grew at the same rate, and value-added tax rates also rose.

Because consumption is a declining fraction of income, it is natural to expect the ratio of value-added tax to income to decline with income. The German Institute for Economic Research in Berlin has repeatedly

3. The present tax rate of 13 percent really amounts to an effective tax rate of 11.5 percent. The official rate applies to value net of tax. The burden faced by consumers is the official rate divided by actual prices, which include tax. Thus the burden is $0.13/1.13 = 0.1150$.

4. For a discussion of the microeconomic and macroeconomic theories of tax shifting, see Dieter Pohmer, "Wirkungen finanzpolitischer Instrumente" (Effects of Financial-Political Instruments), in *Handbuch der Finanzwissenschaft* (Handbook of Public Finance), edited by Fritz Neumark, with the assistance of Norbert Andel and Heinz Haller (Tübingen: J. C. B. Mohr, 1977), vol. 1, pp. 193–346.

contradicted this assumption. Because of the exemption of residential rent and the reduced rate on food, value-added tax burdens are proportional to income.[5] The Ministry of Finance endorses this view.[6] The Rhenish-Westphalian Institute for Economic Research holds the more traditional view that the value-added tax is strongly regressive with respect to income, particularly in the upper income range.[7]

The truth probably lies in the middle; exemptions and reduced rates assure proportionality or even progressivity in the lower income ranges, but the decline in the fraction of income consumed assures regressivity with respect to income in the upper ranges.

Border adjustments ensure that imported goods are subject to the same rate of value-added tax as equivalent domestic products. They also ensure that foreign consumers will be treated differently from German ones, unless the foreign country happens to have the same tax structure as Germany. Some U.S. commentators, as well as other foreign trade theorists and public finance experts, regard all border adjustments as a kind of dumping. Because, they argue, border adjustments are allowed for the value-added tax but not for personal or corporation income taxes, exports from countries that impose income taxes will produce incomes subject to tax in the exporting country and the products will be subject to value-added tax in the importing country. According to some experts, floating exchange rates ensure that most of these effects will be absorbed by exchange rate adjustments which assure equilibrium in the balance of payments, but there may be some changes

5. See Deutsches Institut für Wirtschaftsforschung, "Die Belastung der privaten Haushalte mit indirekten Steuern" (The Burden of Indirect Taxes on Private Households), in *Wochenbericht des DIW* (Weekly Report of the DIW), no. 44 (Berlin, 1977), pp. 377–84; and "Wirken Indirekte Steuern Regressiv? Die Belastung der Privaten Haushalte mit Indirekten Steuern" (Are Indirect Taxes Regressive? The Burden of Indirect Taxes on Private Households), in *Wochenbericht des DIW,* no. 21 (Berlin, 1972), pp. 187–94.

6. See Presse- und Informationsamt der Bundesregierung, "Auswirkungen der zum 1. Januar 1977 geplanten Steuererhöhungen" (Effects of the Planned Increases of Tax on January 1, 1977), in *Aktuelle Beiträge zur Wirtschafts- und Finanzpolitik* (Actual Contributions to Economic and Financial Policy), no. 15 (1976), pp. 1–6, especially p. 3.

7. See Wolfgang Kitterer, "Die Belastung der privaten Haushalte mit indirekten Steuern" (The Burden of Indirect Taxes on Private Households), *Mitteilungen des Rheinisch-Westfälischen Instituts für Wirtschaftsforschung,* vol. 29 (Essen, 1978), pp. 263–80.

in the export and import mix.[8] But structural changes are really unavoidable whenever the public sector takes steps that in any way alter private transactions. As a rule, government demand substitutes for private demand, but occasionally, in financing transfer payments, private demand can be substituted as well. Under personal and corporation income taxation, the demand of taxed persons and corporations is supposed to be restrained by lowering their disposable income. Under value-added taxation, the same effect is supposed to be obtained by an inflationary price increase, which curtails consumers' real income.[9]

Administration

The switch to the value-added tax was smoother administratively than many taxpayers and civil servants expected. Despite certain problems of detail, the basic structure of the value-added tax is simple.

The transition from the gross turnover tax to the value-added tax required some changes in administration. Regulations covering the itemization of tax in invoices had to be developed. The legislature had to make provision for the conversion of long-term private contracts. The temporary investment tax, mentioned above, had to be developed.

The adjustments required of taxpayers were somewhat more significant, most notably in the way accounts were kept and bills rendered, because the new tax required scrupulous attention to the amount of tax levied on a transaction. In many cases, partners in long-term contracts had to bargain over adjustment of the terms. Finally, to make sure that inventories on hand at the time the value-added tax went into effect were zero rated, it was necessary to calculate a fictitious input "tax" on them in order to remove the former turnover tax charges from those economic inputs.

The cost of collecting the value-added tax is modest for the govern-

8. On this subject, see Rolf Peffekoven, "The Destination Principle and Origin Principle and Taxation in International Trade," *German Economic Review,* vol. 12, no. 4 (1974), pp. 281–301; and Rolf Peffekoven, "Die Besteuerung des internationalen Handels" (The Taxation of International Trade), in *Wirtschaftswissenschaftliches Studium* (Studies in Economic Science), vol. 7 (1978), pp. 163–69.

9. For a fuller exposition of these views, see Dieter Pohmer, "Zum Grenzausgleich bei der Umsatzsteuer" (Border Tax Adjustment of the Turnover Tax), in Peter Bohley and Georg Tolkemitt, eds., *Wirtschaftswissenschaft als Grundlage staatlichen Handelns: Heinz Haller zum 65. Geburtstag* (Economics as Foundation of Public Activity) (Tübingen: J. C. B. Mohr, 1979), pp. 249–79.

ment, in part because the tax is entirely self-assessed and failure to file is prosecutable as tax evasion. In general, the tax administration relies on sample checks to assure compliance, but taxpayers with a record of irregularities are subject to closer scrutiny. The sample audits yield considerable information of value in enforcing personal and corporation income taxes as well. But the authorities are hampered by a shortage of personnel in carrying out as many audits as they would like.

One problem in the administration of the value-added tax, unique to Germany in the European Economic Community, has considerable relevance for the United States. Like the United States, Germany is a federal state. Proceeds of the value-added tax are shared between the federation and the *Länder*, or states. The states' portion is based not on local receipts but on population. As a result, the sharing of the proceeds of the value-added tax redistributes income to the poorer states from the richer states. The provisions under which revenues are allotted are determined according to the constitution by a law that until the present time has usually been decreed for a two-year period. The task is complicated by the facts that the allotment provisions must be approved by both houses of the legislature, each is headed by a different political party, and the interests of the federation and the *Länder,* represented in the Bundesrat, diverge. The distribution of revenues is the most controversial aspect of the value-added tax at present.

For most businessmen, the cost of administering the value-added tax is also low. The most troublesome problems involve the need to distinguish between deductible and nondeductible input taxes when some outputs are taxable and some are exempt. Another problem compounds the difficulty some firms face over whether to waive exempt status, a waiver that lasts for several years and thus entails some uncertainty.

The burdens under a value-added tax are distributed in the same way as those under a retail sales tax (which may be regarded as a gross turnover tax levied only on sales by taxable businesses to nontaxable persons).[10] This gives rise to the question, would not a retail sales tax be simpler to administer than the value-added tax? If the bases are similarly defined, the most important difference between them in a federal nation such as Germany is the difference in the regional distribution of accruals.

10. This similarity holds only if services are treated equivalently. In fact, sales taxes in the United States cover services incompletely and variably across the states. See John F. Due, *State and Local Sales Taxation: Structure and Administration* (Chicago: Public Administration Service, 1971), pp. 266–305.

Because the collection of a retail sales tax is close to the site of consumption, it is a suitable local or state consumption tax, whereas the distribution of value-added tax collections is not closely related to the site of consumption. Furthermore, a retail sales tax is irrelevant to transactions between taxable businesses, a feature that eliminates the need for border adjustments of tax liabilities in sales between businesses.

The retail sales tax, however, suffers from a number of decisive disadvantages. First, the value-added tax requires the purchaser to show that he deserves a credit for prior-stage taxes, while the retail sales tax places that responsibility on the seller. In many cases, it is difficult or impossible for the seller to prove that he has sold a product to an exempt purchaser; it is far easier for the purchaser to make this showing. Second, enforcement of tax collections from small businesses poses special difficulties that increase with the tax rate. In general, psychological resistance and evasion increase with tax rates. Because the value-added tax is collected in stages rather than in one lump at the retail stage and because small business is still relatively widespread in Germany at the retail stage, the value-added tax presents fewer enforcement problems than the retail sales tax.

Compared with the personal or corporation income tax, the value-added tax of the consumption type offers the important advantage of eliminating the need to account for depreciation; personal characteristics of taxpayers do not directly affect indirect tax liabilities, but the personal income or consumption tax, which relates more closely to ability to pay, is harder to administer.

Conclusion

German lessons with the value-added tax should not be applied indiscriminately to debates in the United States about the advisability of adopting such a tax. The most important difference is that the value-added tax replaced a well-established gross turnover tax which has no counterpart in the United States. And some of the transitional difficulties that Germany encountered would not be experienced in the United States. On the other hand, German tax administrators and taxpayers had had many years of experience with a tax levied on business at all levels of production. Because the revenue of the new tax closely approximated revenue under the old one, the switch caused little or no inflation. The introduction in the United States of a value-added tax at rates now levied in Germany is hard to imagine. The present rate of 13 percent—or even the 10 percent rate at which the tax was first imposed—could be expected to add to inflationary pressure. For this reason, if the tax were to be introduced, it would be advisable to start at a low rate, perhaps 3 to 5 percent, and then to increase rates little by little.

Some think that it is possible to reduce or to replace the corporation income tax with a value-added tax. This switch is difficult to analyze because the incidence of the corporation income tax is especially controversial; I do not think that in Germany this tax could be shifted onto the consumer. Therefore, an increase in the value-added tax coupled with a reduction of the corporation income tax would have been inflationary in Germany, and such a switch was never contemplated.

Conference Participants

with their affiliations at the time of the conference

Henry J. Aaron *Brookings Institution*

Jean-Pierre Balladur *Ministère du Budget, France*

Kul Bhatia *University of Western Ontario*

David F. Bradford *Princeton University*

Gerard M. Brannon *American Council on Life Insurance*

George F. Break *University of California, Berkeley*

E. Cary Brown *Massachusetts Institute of Technology*

George N. Carlson *U.S. Treasury Department*

Robert M. Clark *University of British Columbia*

Sijbren Cnossen *Erasmus University of Rotterdam*

Antoine Coutière *Ministère de l'Economie, France*

Bruce F. Davie *House Committee on Ways and Means*

D. G. M. Dosser *University of York*

John F. Due *University of Illinois, Urbana*

Francesco Forte *University of Torino*

Joseph Gabbay *Ministry of Finance, Israel*

Richard Goode *International Monetary Fund*

Harry G. Gourevitch *Congressional Research Service*

Richard Hemming *Institute for Fiscal Studies, London*

Richard A. Hoefs *Arthur Andersen and Company*

John A. Kay *Institute for Fiscal Studies, London*

R. W. Lindholm *University of Oregon*

Robert Gerald Livingston *German Marshall Fund*

Paul R. McDaniel *Boston College*

Charles E. McLure, Jr. *National Bureau of Economic Research*

Joseph J. Minarik *Brookings Institution*

Peggy B. Musgrave *University of California, Santa Cruz*

Leif Muten *International Monetary Fund*

Göran Normann *Industrial Institute of Economic and Social Research, Stockholm*

Oliver Oldman *Harvard University*

Joseph A. Pechman *Brookings Institution*

Antonio Pedone *University of Rome*

Rudolph G. Penner *American Enterprise Institute*

Jean-Jacques Philippe *University of Paris I*

Dieter Pohmer *University of Tübingen*

Alan R. Prest *London School of Economics*

C. T. Sandford *University of Bath*

Carl S. Shoup *Sandwich, New Hampshire*

Emil M. Sunley, Jr. *U.S. Treasury Department*

Stanley S. Surrey *Harvard University*

Johannes Weitenberg *Central Planning Bureau, The Hague*

C. C. von Weizsacker *Institute for Sociology and Economics, Bonn*

James W. Wetzler *Joint Committee on Taxation*

Aharon Yoran *Hebrew University, Jerusalem*

Index